Borders, Bindings & Edges

The Art of Finishing Your Quilt

Sally Collins

C&T PUBLISHING

Text and Artwork ©2004 Sally Collins

Artwork ©2004 C&T Publishing

EDITOR: Liz Aneloski

TECHNICAL EDITORS: Sara Kate MacFarland and Joyce Engels Lytle

COPYEDITOR/PROOFREADER: Stacy Chamness/Eva Simoni Erb

ILLUSTRATORS: Jeff Carrillo and Matt Allen

COVER DESIGNER: Kristy Konitzer

DESIGN DIRECTOR/BOOK DESIGNER: Rose Sheifer

PRODUCTION ASSISTANT: Matt Allen

QUILT HOW-TO PHOTOGRAPHY: Diane Pedersen

PHOTOGRAPHY: Sharon Risedorph, unless otherwise noted

Published by C&T Publishing, Inc., P.O. Box 1456, Lafayette, California, 94549

FRONT COVER: *Crossroads*

Attention Teachers: C&T Publishing, Inc. encourages you to use this book as a text for teaching. Contact us at 800-284-1114 or www.ctpub.com for more information about the C&T Teachers Program.

We take great care to ensure that the information included in this book is accurate and presented in good faith, but no warranty is provided nor results guaranteed. Having no control over the choices of materials or procedures used, neither the author nor C&T Publishing, Inc. shall have any liability to any person or entity with respect to any loss or damage caused directly or indirectly by the information contained in this book. For your convenience, we post an up-to-date listing of corrections on our website (www.ctpub.com). If a correction is not already noted, please contact our customer service department at ctinfo@ctpub.com or at P.O. Box 1456, Lafayette, California, 94549.

Trademarked (™) and Registered Trademark (®) names are used throughout this book. Rather than use the symbols with every occurrence of a trademark and registered trademark name, we are using the names only in the editorial fashion and to the benefit of the owner, with no intention of infringement.

Library of Congress Cataloging-in-Publication Data

Collins, Sally.
Borders, bindings & edges : the art of finishing your quilt / Sally Collins.
    p. cm.
Includes bibliographical references and index.
 ISBN 1-57120-233-1 (Paper trade)
1. Quilting. 2. Borders, Ornamental Decorative arts) I. Title.
TT835.C6473963 2004
746.46--dc22
                        2003023422

10 9 8 7 6 5 4 3 2 1

CONTENTS

Dedication

To all the quilters who have taken my classes over the past twenty years, I sincerely thank you for continually encouraging my efforts, inspiring me to grow, learn, and move forward, and for always appreciating my work. I am forever grateful to you all.

Acknowledgments

Writing books is never a solo effort and I have had the assistance and help of many generous people:
The gracious contributors of beautiful quilts, Nancy Rink, Cynthia Sherburne, Nadine Thompson, Judy Mathieson, Laura Nownes, Diana McClun, and The Modesto Quilt Guild. The talented machine-quilting contributors, Don Linn, Jill Schumacher, Kathleen Pappas, and Cindy Young.
The C&T Staff who make the dream reality: Liz Aneloski, editor, friend, and the person who freely gave her expertise and knowledge to bring order to my words; Sara Kate MacFarland, my technical editor; Diane Pedersen for her artistic and how-to photographic skills; and Sharon Risedorph for her beautiful quilt photographs.
And to my husband Joe, for his unconditional love.
This book would not exist without their support, encouragement, knowledge, and faith in my vision for this book. I thank you all, from the bottom of my heart.

INTRODUCTION

In the past, quilts were primarily made for our beds, to keep us warm and add color and pattern to our surroundings. Most often, the border's purpose was to add size. Bias binding was then applied to add durability.

Although we continue to make bed quilts, for many of us, our preference has shifted to smaller quilts that are produced for display and viewing pleasure. The scale and proportion of these quilts is smaller than bed quilts, which means that the viewer sees the central design area, the border area, and the final edge all at once, like a piece of art in a gallery. Therefore, the visual impact is immediate. The border and edge bear more responsibility for the success of the quilt and have more importance.

Borders and edges are design elements, not simply afterthoughts. This does not mean they need to be complicated or difficult to accomplish. Borders and edges should serve as a frame for the quilt center; to enrich, complement, strengthen, and support the central design. Integrating the quilt design with the border area and edge is key to creating a visually successful wall quilt. The border and edge should add significant detail and create a seamless, organized arrangement of all the elements that engage the attention of the viewer.

I will share my philosophy on choosing, designing, coloring, and applying borders and edge finishes to traditional-style wall quilts. I will offer my perspective and suggestions to the many questions we all encounter when it comes time to add borders to our quilts. Does my quilt need a border? What style should I use (plain fabric, pieced, appliqué, border print, or some combination of those)? How do I figure out the right size and proportion? What should the total border area be? How do I figure out how to make my border fit my quilt? How many borders should I add? What colors and fabrics should I use? Should I curve the edge or leave it straight? Do I use bias, straight-grain, double-fold or single-fold binding? The list goes on and on! There is much to consider when planning and executing the final touches to our quilts, taking adequate time is well worth the effort.

First Quilt, 1978, machine pieced by author, machine quilted by Stover Quality Quilting. My son's sampler quilt is surrounded by plain fabric borders to make it fit the bed, typical of the time.

I encourage you to read through the entire book before adding a border or edge finish to your next quilt.

Creative and interesting borders and edge finishes do not need to be complicated or difficult to be beautiful. Often, the most simple of choices can achieve the desired effect. Join me as I explore and share opportunities and choices, which will bring your next quilt to a beautiful conclusion!

Piece
Sally

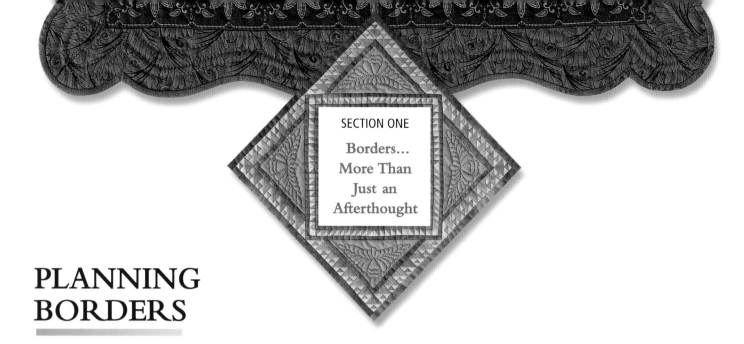

PLANNING BORDERS

Purpose and Function

Borders are the visual conclusion of a quilt. They should enhance, support, contain, and frame the central design; they can echo, reinforce, repeat, and unify the design elements already present in the quilt (i.e., shape, color, and fabric) and contribute to the overall balance and rhythm of the quilt. Borders can expand the central design by extending an element of the quilt center into the border area. They can serve as a bridge that helps the eye move from the central design to the edge, creating a smooth transition and providing a resting place for the eye. Borders can add size, or serve as a simple frame to stop and contain a busy design. They can be an area to display beautiful quilting or to add appliqué or piecing that relates to the central design. Borders can establish the dominant color of a quilt, add interest, and bring organization to the arrangement of shapes and colors. Borders should not overpower, compete with, or draw attention away from the central design. And not all quilts need a border to be visually complete.

The objective and goal of a border can change from quilt to quilt. As your quilt progresses toward completion ask yourself, "Does this addition make my quilt better?" If not, stop and question what you are adding and perhaps why. Maybe it is a good idea but the proportion or color is off. Do not go forward until you are improving your quilt. Careful planning and exploration of all border options will result in a quilt that is unified and complete.

Choosing a Border

Borders play an important, co-starring role in the total visual impact and success of wall quilts. They should enhance and complement the central design without creating a distraction.

There are three basic border styles (use singly or in combination):

- single or multiple plain-fabric borders
- appliqué borders
- pieced borders

Joe's Log Cabin, 1993, machine pieced and quilted by author, Half Log Cabin block design by Sharyn Craig of El Cajon, CA. Complete in itself, no border was needed.

Five-Patch Sampler, 2002, designed, machine pieced, and hand quilted by author. Multiple techniques (narrow, dogtooth, double sawtooth) precede the final boxed plain border. If your central design has lots of triangles you might choose a sawtooth border, or perhaps a double row of sawteeth.

Look through quilt books, magazines, and photos of quilts from shows. Catalogs that show floor rugs or picture frames are also an idea resource. Keep the pages and notes in a file for future reference. Review the bibliography (page 112) for additional books on borders. One in particular that I constantly use for design ideas is *The Grammar of Ornament* by Owen Jones (1987, Dover Publications, Inc.). How or if you plan to quilt in the border will also influence your choices.

I wait until the central design is complete before making a final choice of borders. I might have ideas initially, but the planning and choosing is put off until its time. Waiting gives the quilt time to develop a voice and gives me time to listen.

Sedona, 2001, designed, machine pieced, and hand quilted by author. Simplicity at its best, a sawtooth border combined with plain fabric borders frame the center star design.

Ruler-Friendly Numbers

Ruler-friendly numbers are ones easily found on rotary cutting rulers. When the math process for figuring out shape sizes for cutting results in numbers smaller than ⅛", I make templates. When using the calculator to figure sizes, the result is in tenths. Look three places to the right of the decimal point and then refer to the Decimal Equivalent Chart on page 62 if needed. If anything smaller than an eighth results, round off the decimal to the nearest tenth, draw the shape on 10-to-the-inch graph paper, add ¼" seam allowance on all sides of each shape, and make a template.

Proportion and Scale

Proportion and scale relate to:

- Total width of the border area
- Size of the individual shapes used in the border when piecing or appliquéing

To be successful, the border composition must be proportionate to the center design in size and scale. There is no formula to follow to know how wide the total border area should be. Trust your own good judgment. One guideline that can be used as a starting point is the block size, but this is only an option if you are breaking up that space into multiple borders. A quilt with 12" blocks would look poorly designed with one big 12"-wide fabric strip as its only border. When designing medallion quilts, the border width might be 20–25% of the center design. Work on paper and draw to scale, a border the total width you think your quilt can accommodate, then break up the space within it.

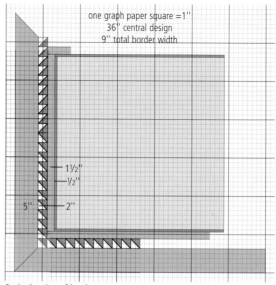

one graph paper square =1"
36" central design
9" total border width

1½"
½"
5" 2"

Scale drawing of border

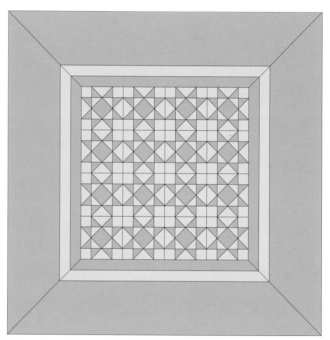

Total border width is too wide and overwhelming

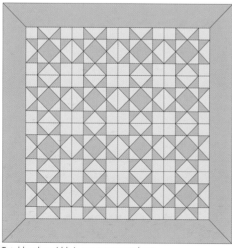

Total border width is too narrow and can look incomplete and unfinished

Garden Gate, 2003, designed and machine pieced by author, machine quilted by Don Linn of Redding, CA. Adding an automatic-fit repeat-block border in half the size of the interior blocks adds detail and elegance to a simple traditional Monkey Wrench design. Central block size and total width of border are similar.

Detail of **Crossroad** (full quilt page 65). Sawtooth border triangles are half the size (¾") used in center block (1½").

Proportion and scale relative to shape size also requires careful consideration. To keep the eye focused toward the center, the size of the pieced or appliqué shapes in the border should be smaller (in most cases) than the shapes used in the central design. My experience has been that if I use the same size shapes, they compete for attention with the center and the eye tends to bounce back and forth from the center to the border as if it cannot make up its mind where to look. Choose a size that divides evenly into the size of the center shape to create an automatic fit (page 63).

When you view your quilt, your eye should be initially captured by the center design and then travel out to the border. When the border's total width and individual shape size looks right and seems balanced to you, it is.

Starry Night, 1996, designed, pieced, and quilted by Cynthia Sherburne, Portland, OR. A double sawtooth border repeats the shape of the stars and two sizes adds detail. If using two different sizes of shapes, one should be the same and one smaller (three-quarters or one-half the size used for the center).

Hearts, 1985-2003, designed and pieced by author, inspired by a Moneca Calvert design class. Machine quilted by Don Linn of Redding, CA. The pieced hearts were a perfect candidate for a pieced ribbon border and the addition of a light final border allows the entire design to float. Rounded corners and a piping/binding combination finish the edge. A light, final border also creates an airy, openness.

Color and Fabric

Good design is a result of carefully mixing and blending design elements (value, color, texture, shape or form, line, scale, and direction) to create a harmonious, balanced quilt. Creating a harmonious, balanced quilt requires both unity and variety. Unity holds a quilt design together and provides some visual organization through repetition of the design elements. Variety prevents monotony, creates interest, and enhances the design.

Color

Quilts benefit from repeating the colors that have already been established in the central design and variety is achieved by changing some of the values (lighter or darker), intensities (muted or bright) of the colors and/or fabric prints (visual texture) used in the central design. Both repetition and variety of color and fabric print will create a smooth, unified, balanced, successful border. In most cases, introducing a new, unrelated color in the border can create confusion and become a distraction.

The color you choose for the final plain-fabric border (if one is used) will greatly influence the color of the entire quilt and become dominant. It will also cause your eye to notice and find that color wherever it appears in the quilt. If you add a blue final border to a multi-colored scrappy quilt, for example, the quilt will be recognized as a "blue" quilt. Choose carefully.

If you have used a light color in the central design area, repeating it in a narrow ⅛"-¼" border helps to connect the two areas, adds a halo-type effect, and can prevent the border from getting too dark. Generally speaking, darker-colored borders contain and frame the quilt and draw the eye inward. The exception to this (and there are always exceptions) is often found on appliqué-style quilts that have quilt designs that float on light backgrounds.

Detail of **Sophisticated Sampler** If a color is too strong, use only half of that color combined with another color that quiets the strong one, as I did using the small gold squares to quiet the orange ones.

Repetitive Sequence

Detail of **Medallion Sampler** (full quilt page 71). Random sampling of fabrics in a repetitive sequence.

Continuity with the color in borders is also important. Referring to *Crossroad* on page 65, notice that the triangles in the center block are both burgundy and blue. Since there were more blue triangles in the center block than burgundy, using all blue sawtooth triangles in the border provided continuity and a smoothness that contributed to the oneness of the design. I did some rough-cut mock-ups on my design wall to "see" how different options would look so I could make a more informed decision, rather than guess. Take the time necessary to compose and design your quilt's border carefully. Refer to Design Process beginning on page 66, for more detailed information.

PLANNED RANDOM

When planning a scrappy pieced border, choose a random sampling of the fabrics and colors from the central design, perhaps nine. Cut a small piece of each fabric, arrange them in a pleasing sequence, and number them 1 through 9. You can arrange them in a repetitive sequence 1 through 9, 1 through 9 and so on, or arrange 1 through 9, then 8 through 1, then 2 through 9, then 8 through 1 and so on. This is also a very effective way to organize the fabrics if you are sequencing the color by value, light to dark, or the reverse.

Fabric

I use good quality, 100% cotton fabric, prewash all my fabrics, and cut plain-fabric borders from the lengthwise grain whenever possible. The lengthwise grain has virtually no stretch and therefore helps create a stable, straight border. Visual texture (stripe, floral, dots, checks, etc.) plays a large role in the success of a quilt's design.

Large florals can also create beautiful texture, add interest, and soften the straight lines of geometric piecing.

Repeating fabrics from the central design in the border will create balance and continuity in the whole design. You can change fabrics, but do so carefully and be sure they make sense and relate. Keeping the color the same but changing the visual texture works because they relate. The plaid fabric used for the final border in *Sedona* (page 7) was never used in the central design but it works because it uses all the colors used in the center. The same is true for *Paws and Reflect* on page 70. The teal outer border fabric was never used in the central border design.

Sophisticated Sampler, 2003, designed and machine pieced by author, machine quilted by Jill Schumacher of Weed, CA. This sampler-style quilt uses a border print repeatedly, to add texture and detail. A chain of squares, an outlined dogtooth border, and a final mitered border complete the design. A stripe and a border print can sometimes fill the need of a pieced border.

If you based your color palette and border on a multi-colored border fabric chosen early in the process, be sure it is still appropriate for a border and improves your quilt at the end of the process. You are not required to use it. It can serve solely as a palette.

If you run out of a fabric, try to find one that is similar in color and value. The substitutions and changes shouldn't be terribly obvious and distracting; instead, they should be interesting and friendly with the other fabrics.

Keep in mind that solid and quiet tone-on-tone fabrics expose and show off elaborate, intricate quilting designs, whereas busy prints do not.

Scale Drawings

Grid refers to the number of equal divisions down and across a block that enables you to draft it. Graph paper *squares* are the individual small squares on graph paper that are eventually assigned a size (one graph square equals 1", for example) that enables you to design proportionally and know what size to cut shapes for sewing.

The grid can appear along the edge of a block or along a long seam inside the block area. The smallest piece is usually the basis for the grid.

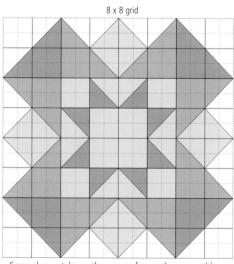

8 x 8 grid

Some shapes take up the space of more than one grid.

A scale drawing is a small, proportional representation of a block or quilt design. Once a size is assigned to each graph paper square (1" or ¾" or 2") the drawing becomes a map with information to create the whole quilt.

If the design is symmetrical, you only need a section (a quarter or an eighth). In that case, mirrors can be used to see the whole design.

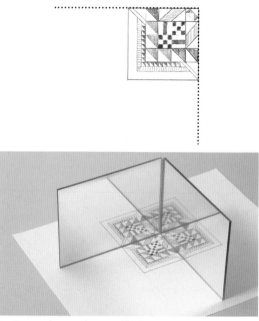

Drawing to scale on graph paper, with mirrors

Reasons for making a full or partial scale drawing:

- to evaluate proportion, scale, and design
- to make decisions by using mirrors to view the whole design
- to allow new ideas or serendipity to occur
- to experiment with color
- to determine the size of the shapes to cut (after adding seam allowance)
- to create custom borders and their corner connections
- to see the quilt oriented on point or on square
- for piecing and assembly information

You can use different graph papers, although 8- or 10-to-the-inch will be most useful. Once the grid is identified, go to the appropriate graph paper and draw the block following the grid. You can draw the block on square or on point. When sketching, you do not need to worry about the size of the scale. If your block grid is different from your border grid, draw the central design area on one kind of graph paper, perhaps 10-to-the-inch, cut it out and place it on 8-to-the-inch graph paper to continue designing. When a scale drawing of your design has been created, assign a size to each small graph paper square that then establishes the scale. You can now translate the scale to create actual-size shapes for cutting your fabric.

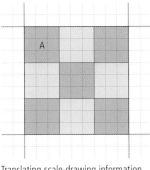

Scale: 1 graph square = 1", 9" Nine-Patch block.

Shape A = 3 graph squares by 3 graph squares = 3" x 3" finished.

Cut Shape A 3½" square for sewing.

Translating scale-drawing information to cutting

Noteworthy

You must always draw the shapes you create finished size, then add a ¼" seam allowance to all sides of each shape for cutting size.

Practice making scale drawings to get a clear understanding of how they are created and their importance to the creative and technical process. Take advantage of the information they offer.

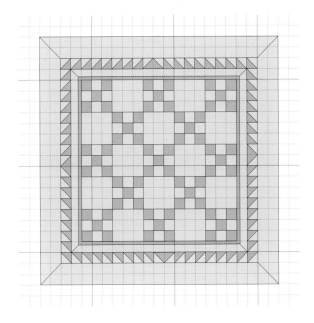

Scale: 1 graph square = 2"
6" Nine-Patch block, Border total = 8"
Sawtooth size = 2"
Quilt size = 46" square

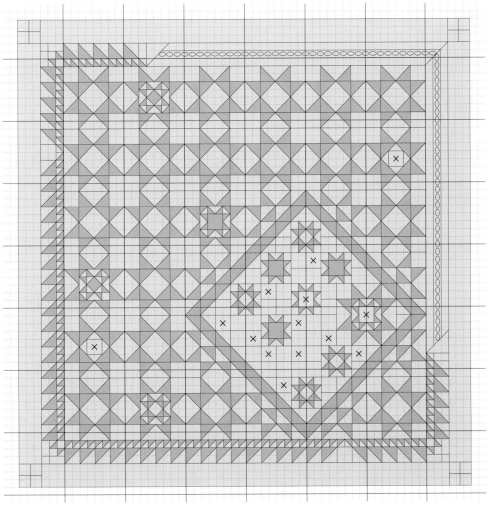

One graph square = ¾"
X = 1½" stars
Quilt size 45" square
Border ¾" and 1½" Sawteeth

Scale drawing of **Stepping Out** on page 77.

Measuring the Quilt for Borders

Taking the time to cut, sew, pin, press, correct, and measure accurately will insure beautifully constructed borders. More detailed information on piecing techniques can be found in my book *The Art of Machine Piecing.*

To figure out how long to cut the borders, measure your quilt vertically (for side borders) and horizontally (for top and bottom borders) across the center, not the edges, since they might have stretched in handling and sewing. The quilt should lie flat and relaxed during measuring. Do not stretch it. If you are using a scale drawing and are within ¼" of those measurements, use those. To cut the width of borders, add ½" seam allowance to the finished width.

On a square quilt, the horizontal and vertical measurements should be the same. If they are not, average them so you work with one number. On a rectangular quilt, the side measurements should be the same as should the top and bottom measurements. The diagonal measurement (this will not be the same measurement as horizontal and vertical) from corner to corner in both directions should also be the same on squares and rectangles and is done only to evaluate squareness. You will not use the diagonal measurements for cutting.

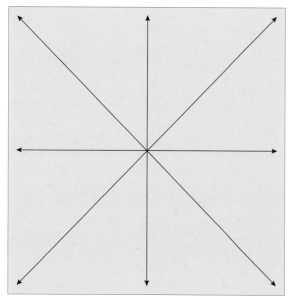

Measure horizontally, vertically, and diagonally.

If your measurements are way off your planned measurements, you can add spacer borders, to your quilt page 24, to bring it up to a more consistent size to accommodate the border style of your choice.

Do I Sew with the Border or the Quilt on Top?

The quilt must fit the borders. It is important that the edges of the quilt fit the borders rather than stretching the borders out to meet the edges of the quilt.

1. If adding an unpieced, plain border to the quilt, place the border on top and the quilt on the bottom, right sides together, because if the quilt top edges are a little longer than the borders, it is important that the fullest of the two fabrics, (in this case the quilt top) be on the bottom, next to the feed dogs, so they can help ease in the fullness.

2. If adding a pieced border or border print to the quilt, place the border on top and the quilt on the bottom, right sides together, because it will be important to see either the intersections when sewing, to create complete shapes and sharp points on a pieced border, or the design lines on a border print.

3. If the quilt top edge has piecing, place the quilt on top and the plain border on the bottom, right sides together, for the same reasons as Step 2 above.

4. If both the border and the quilt top have piecing, they should both measure the same. If they do not, place the fullest one on the bottom, so the feed dogs can help ease in the fullness.

WHOLE-FABRIC BORDERS

Whole-fabric borders can be created from a single strip or multiple strips of solid or printed fabric, or a combination of both. Combining color and visual textures of the same or similar fabrics used in the central design, in varying widths, adds to the complexity and detail of the quilt.

Using a single strip of printed fabric can be very interesting and beautiful and would most often benefit from being mitered at the corners to give a more formal look and, in the case of a border print, continue the design uninterrupted. See Border-Print Fabric Borders beginning on page 26. A single width of solid or tone-on-tone fabric can also be very effective if you are planning to quilt a beautiful, intricate design. A busy fabric print will not show off quilting designs, as well as a solid. The width of a single or multiple whole-fabric border should be proportionate to the central design; refer to Proportion and Scale beginning on page 8.

When interviewing fabric for a single or multiple whole-fabric border, first decide the total width of the border.

If multiple strips of fabric are the plan, first go to graph paper, draw the total border width and begin to break up the space into various widths. It is usually more appealing to graduate the widths from narrow to wide for the more significant fabrics, and use very narrow borders (⅛", ¼" or ⅜") to separate them. Including the narrow borders is an opportunity to add a little bit of a very dark, hot, or intense color and create design detail with minimal effort. The graph paper aids planning, but always remain open to change. For example, if the total width of the border is 4", I might break up that area into five borders, ⅜" + ¼" + ½" + ⅛" + 2¾" = 4" total.

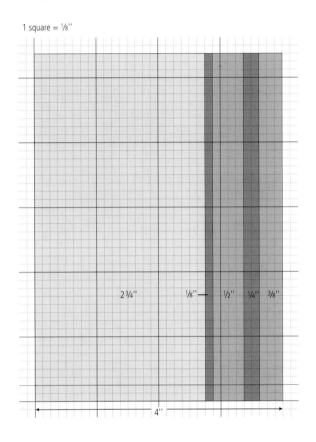

1 square = ⅛"

2¾" ⅛"— ½" ¼" ⅜"

4"

Using the graph paper as a map, choose fabrics and fold them to expose the finished width, then lay or pin them next to your quilt to interview, using a mirror or instant photos. Evaluate, examine, rearrange, and change until you find an arrangement of width, color, and fabric print that best serves the quilt.

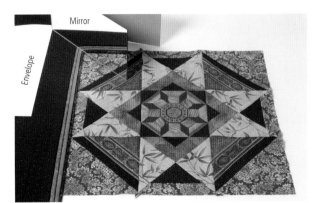

Mirror

Envelope

Interviewing multiple-fabric borders using a mirror

Quilts that have very complex, busy central designs can often benefit from a simple frame that stops the design, quiets the chaos, and allows the eye to rest.

Adding Borders to the Quilt Top

1. Measure the quilt top (page 16) and cut the border strips as instructed in the individual corner treatment instructions that follow. When necessary, join border strips diagonally to create the required length, unless you are joining border prints or stripes.

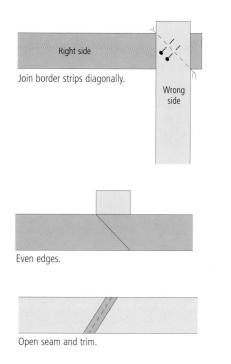

Join border strips diagonally.

Even edges.

Open seam and trim.

2. Align the edges of one of the border strips with the quilt top exactly. First pin (perpendicular) the center and ends of the border strip to the center and corners of the quilt top, then add additional pins, parallel to the edge, for stable, smooth sewing. Stitch each border to the quilt top with a ¼" seam allowance. Press the stitches, then press the seam allowance toward the outside edge.

Corner Treatments

Whole-fabric borders (single or multiple strips) can be added to your quilt in five different ways. All of these styles affect the corner finish differently. The corner treatment you choose should align with the character of the quilt.

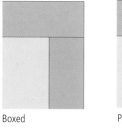

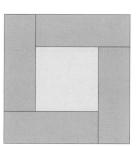

Boxed   Plain or pieced, squared

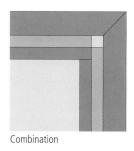

Mitered

Partial seaming

Combination

A border consisting of multiple styles; a pieced border, a couple of narrow borders, and a border print or whole-fabric final border would each have different corner treatments.

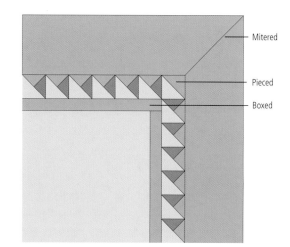

Multiple corner applications within one border

Boxed-Corner Borders

Whether your border consists of one or multiple fabric strips, always add each individual fabric by first adding the two side borders, then the top and bottom borders of each fabric, maintaining a 90° corner. See page 16 to measure and cut the side borders. Add them to the quilt. Measure horizontally including the side borders to determine the length of the top and bottom borders.

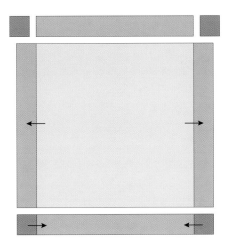

Add sides, then top and bottom.

Squared-Corner Borders, Plain or Pieced

This type of border contains a square in each corner. The corner square is the size of the total finished width of the border and can be the same fabric, a different fabric, or pieced. The border can be one fabric or multiple strips of varying widths, all sewn together to create a strip unit that is added to the quilt as one border. After you have decided the total width of the border, work on graph paper if you plan to join multiple widths of fabric strips to make up a strip unit. See page 16 to measure for borders. Do all measuring and cutting before adding the borders to the quilt.

For a square quilt, all four borders (one fabric or multiple strips) are cut the same length by the desired finished width, plus ½" for seam allowance.

The four corner squares must be the same size as the finished width of the borders, plus ½" seam allowance. Add two borders to the sides of the quilt top (see Adding Borders to the Quilt Top, Step 2, page 18). Sew a square to each end of the remaining two borders and press the seam allowances away from the corners. Add to the top and bottom of the quilt top.

Mitered-Corner Borders

Borders with mitered corners add grace and symmetry when using a striped fabric, border-print fabric, or multiple strips of plain, unpieced fabric.

Fabric styles that benefit from mitering

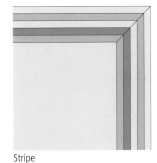

Stripe

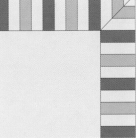

Stripe

Border print

Multiple whole-fabric borders

Mitered corners can appear complex and require a little more fabric than other border styles but the results are well worth the effort. Their Y-seam construction takes a little more time, but is not difficult.

To add a single-fabric border and miter the corners:

1. Measure your square quilt (page 16). Cut each border strip to this measurement plus twice the width of the unfinished border, adding another 6" for insurance. For example, 60½" (quilt size) + 9" (twice a 4½" border) + 6" (extra) = 75½" (border strip). A rectangular quilt will have two different measurements.

2. On the wrong side of your quilt top, place a pin at the center of all four sides of your quilt and mark a dot ¼" from each edge at the four corners.

3. Fold each border strip in half to find the center and place a pin at this point. Measure out from the center pin in both directions, half the finished measurement of the side of the quilt it will be sewn to (30").

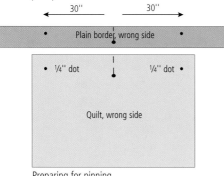

Preparing for pinning

4. Place the border strip and the quilt top, right sides together, quilt on the bottom, and match center pins, and corner dots. Align the edges exactly, add additional pins, positioned parallel to the edge.

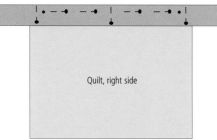
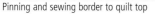

Pinning and sewing border to quilt top

5. Sew the border onto the quilt top, beginning just in front of the dot, take three stitches, backstitch, then continue to the other corner dot, stopping just in front of the dot and backstitch three stitches. Press the seam to the outer edge of the quilt.

6. Repeat for the remaining three borders and miter the corners by hand or machine as described in Border-Print, Fabric Borders on pages 31–32.

To add a multiple-strip border and miter the corners, join the strips of fabric together and treat as one border following the instructions above.

Partial-Seam-Corner Borders

Partial-seam borders can add a whimsical quality to quilts, especially if you change colors and/or prints for each border. A striped fabric can add motion and direction.

1. Measure your quilt (page 16).
2. Subtract ½" for seam allowance.
3. Add the desired finished width of one border to the length.
4. Add the ½" seam allowance back in.
5. Cut all four borders for a square quilt that exact length by the desired finished width plus ½" for seam allowance. For example, your quilt measures 60½" square minus ½" equals 60", plus 4" for one finished border width, equals 64" plus ½" seam allowance. All four borders would be cut 64½" long and 4½" wide. Always work with finished measurements and add ½" seam allowance last. For rectangular quilts, the two side borders would be the same and the top and bottom borders would be the same.
6. Working counterclockwise and referring to the illustration, align the first border with the top of the quilt and sew only a few inches. Attach the second border. Press to set the stitches and press the seam allowance toward the border.
7. Add the remaining borders and press as above.
8. Complete the partial seam. Press toward the border.

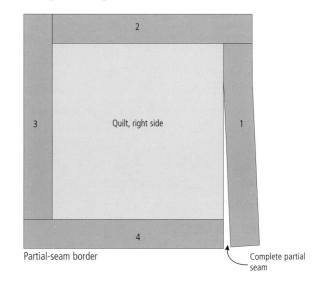

Partial-seam border

Complete partial seam

Striped-Fabric Borders

You can apply a striped-fabric border with a boxed corner, mitered corner, or partial-seam corner. Details on how to measure are on page 16. Cutting and sewing information is found under each individual type of border.

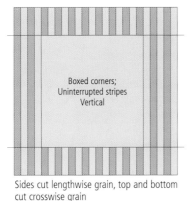

Boxed corners;
Uninterrupted stripes
Vertical

Sides cut lengthwise grain, top and bottom cut crosswise grain

Boxed corners;
Uninterrupted stripes
Horizontal

Sides cut crosswise grain, top and bottom cut lengthwise grain

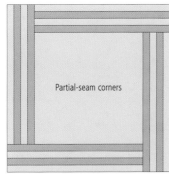

Partial-seam corners

Border cut on lengthwise grain appears to have motion.

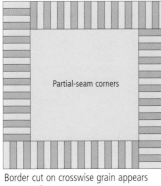

Partial-seam corners

Border cut on crosswise grain appears more static.

To miter a striped fabric that is cut on the crosswise grain, the principle is the same as mitering a corner on a border print fabric (pages 31–32). The exact same part of the print on both sides of the corner to be mitered must be positioned at the mitering point. In most cases, whether your quilt is square or rectangular, this will require a seam in each border strip. Make the straight seam joint as inconspicuous as possible. Refer to Cut and Sew Borders from a Symmetrical Border Print on a Rectanglar Quilt beginning on page 30.

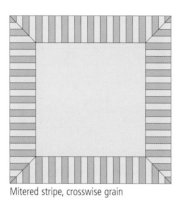

Mitered stripe, crosswise grain

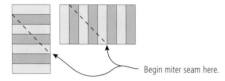

Begin miter seam here.

To miter a striped fabric that is cut on the lengthwise grain, you would treat it the same as you would a multiple-fabric strip border, page 20.

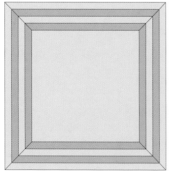

Mitered stripe, lengthwise grain

Very Narrow ⅛" Borders

These borders give unexpected sparkle and detail to quilts. They offer an opportunity to introduce a very hot, dark, or intense color, and can outline and define shapes or whole areas.

By creating a strip unit and templates, this technique can also be used to interrupt side triangles and corners in diagonal sets, or to fracture shapes within patchwork blocks.

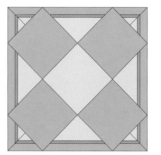

Interrupt side and corner triangles.

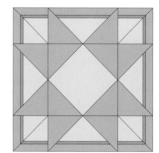

Fracture shapes in blocks.

Ohio Stars, 1997, designed, machine pieced, and hand quilted by author. Narrow borders, border print, and a lovely curved edge complete the simple traditional design.

I originally developed this technique to add proportional border widths to very small or intricate work. I wanted it to be sewn in like a border, rather than a folded piece of fabric (flange) sewn between borders. Over time, the folded strip can look untidy because the fold of the flange is loose and not sewn down, and can get wrinkled when the quilt is folded and unfolded.

You can add these very narrow ⅛" borders to your quilt separately, as you would a boxed corner, or join multiple border strips, including the ⅛" border, then add them to your quilt as one border and miter the corners.

First, oversize the cut width of the border you want to finish ⅛" and the border that follows it by ⅜" for stability while sewing; then, trim the appropriate ¼" seam allowance to an exact ⅛". This cut edge serves as the sewing guide when adding the next border. The success of this technique depends on accurate trimming and sewing very straight, right along the cut edge of the just-trimmed seam allowance. To determine how wide to cut your border strips you must first know how wide the finished width will be. If you want three borders and want to miter the corners, all three will be sewn together to make a strip unit. You can also add these borders separately in a boxed fashion. For example, Border #1 will finish 1" so cut 1½"-wide strips. Border #2 will finish ⅛", so cut 1" wide strips (⅛" + ½" usual seam allowance + ⅜" extra = 1"). Border #3 will finish 2", so cut 2⅞"-wide strips (2"+ ½" usual seam allowance + ⅜" extra = 2⅞" because this border follows the ⅛" border).

1. Using the three borders as an example, sew #1 to #2, right sides together with a ¼" seam allowance. Trim this seam to an exact ⅛". Press to set the stitches, then press the seam allowance toward #2.

2. Place #3 and #1–2 right sides together, with #1–2 on top and edges aligned. Sew along the just-trimmed seam allowance edge. This creates the ⅛" border.

3. Trim the excess to within ¼" from the last line of stitching, press to set the stitches, press seam toward #3.

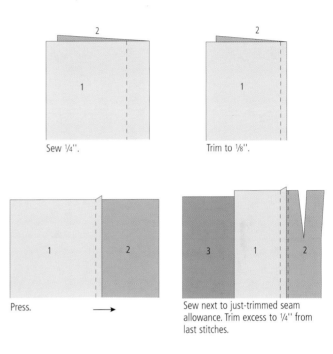

Sew ¼".   Trim to ⅛".

Press. →   Sew next to just-trimmed seam allowance. Trim excess to ¼" from last stitches.

Finished ⅛" border

Spacer Borders

Spacer borders are plain-fabric borders that can be the perfect solution to overcome cutting and/or sewing inaccuracies, to separate one pieced border from another, or to separate, float, and/or isolate the central design from the borders. They can be used to quiet chaotic areas, to emphasize and outline an area, or to introduce a color or fabric. However, spacer borders are most often used to bring a quilt up to a size that accommodates a repeat unit chosen for a pieced or appliqué border.

When adding a pieced border to a quilt, multiples of the repeat-unit size must fit the edge of the quilt exactly. You cannot have a little extra hang over and cut it off!

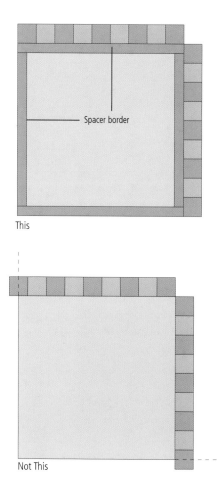

Spacer border

This

Not This

Let's say the quilt measures 60" finished. The finished length of the repeat-unit size of the pieced border is 2". Dividing the side of the quilt by the unit size tells me the number of units needed per side. 60" ÷ 2" = 30 units per side, perfect! Now let's imagine the quilt measures only 58½" finished. A 2" repeat does not divide equally into 58½" (58½" ÷ 2" = 29.25 or 29 whole units and one quarter of another). Here is when a spacer border is necessary to bring the quilt up to a size that accommodates the pieced border repeat unit. The width of a spacer border is half the difference between what the quilt measures finished and what it needs to measure to accommodate the pieced border repeat unit. The next higher number equally divisible by 2" is 60". The difference between 58½" (what the quilt now measures) and 60" (what it needs to measure) is 1½". Half of 1½" is ¾", the finished width of the spacer borders. If you add four ¾" finished spacer borders to your quilt you will bring it up to a 60" square finished. Always add ½" to the finished width when cutting border strips. In this case the border width would be cut 1¼" (¾" + ½" = 1¼").

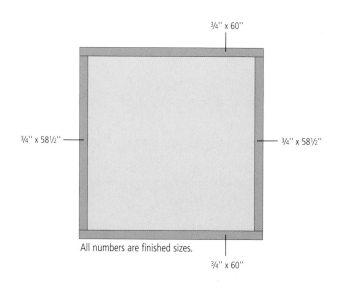

¾" x 60"

¾" x 58½"

¾" x 58½"

All numbers are finished sizes.

¾" x 60"

On a rectangular quilt, using the same 2" pieced border repeat unit as we did for a square quilt, you need to figure out the spacer border dimensions for the length and width of the quilt separately. Sometimes the width of the spacer borders will need to be different for the sides than they are for the top and bottom.

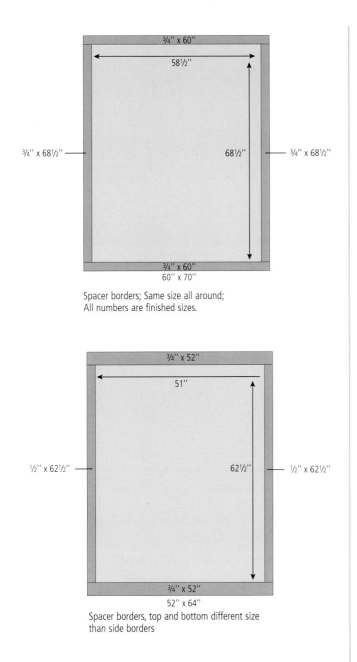

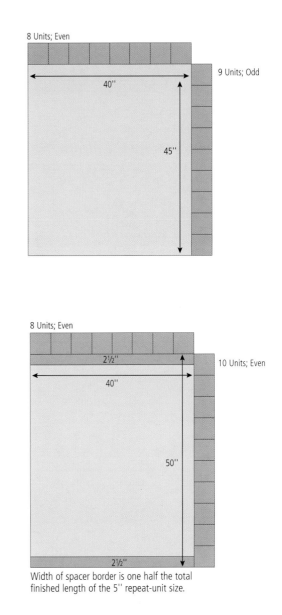

Top left diagram labels:

3/4" x 60"
58½"
3/4" x 68½" 68½" 3/4" x 68½"
3/4" x 60"
60" x 70"

Spacer borders; Same size all around;
All numbers are finished sizes.

Middle left diagram labels:

3/4" x 52"
51"
½" x 62½" 62½" ½" x 62½"
3/4" x 52"
52" x 64"

Spacer borders, top and bottom different size
than side borders

Top right diagram labels:

8 Units; Even
9 Units; Odd
40"
45"

Middle right diagram labels:

8 Units; Even
2½"
10 Units; Even
40"
50"
2½"

Width of spacer border is one half the total
finished length of the 5'' repeat-unit size.

Sometimes the pieced border design requires an even (or odd) number of units on all sides of the quilt. Let's say the quilt measures 40" x 45" finished and we want a 5" repeat unit. The width of the quilt accommodates an even number of repeat units (40" ÷ 5" = 8 units) but the length measurement of the quilt accommodates an odd number of repeat units (45" ÷ 5" = 9 units). In this case, if we want an even number of repeat units on all sides of the quilt, a spacer border needs to be added to the top and bottom of the quilt, one half the total finished length of one repeat unit (half of a 5" unit is 2½"). This allows space for one additional whole unit on the sides of the quilt, changing the total number from odd to even.

Noteworthy

If the purpose of the spacer borders is to adjust the quilt measurements to accommodate a pieced border, make them as narrow as you can successfully sew. Cut them from the same fabric (or one of a similar color and value) that they will touch to make them less conspicuous. Doing this will also disguise using different widths of spacer borders. If the spacer border width gets too wide and conspicuous, you can break up the space into more than one border, allowing additional color, design and fabric opportunities. See *Crossroad* on page 65. The spacer border floats the design and brings it up to a size that accommodates the pieced border in *Star Crossed* (page 72).

BORDER-PRINT FABRIC BORDERS

Border prints are beautiful in their design and color. They have enormous voice and potential for various applications and add detail, sophistication, and elegance to any quilt.

The design on border prints can be totally or partially symmetrical, asymmetrical, or directional, although symmetrical is the easiest to use to create mirror-image corners. Directional border prints can be partially symmetrical and have the potential to create mirror-image corners or they can be asymmetrical.

Use a template to custom cut repeat shapes.

Christmas Rose. 1986–2003. Blocks machine pieced by author and five friends, machine quilted by Cindy Young, Newark, CA. Using both the diamond shape of the Dutch Rose block as a pieced border and the border print for the final border enhances the design. The border-print design is uninterrupted around perimeter.

Detail of **Diamond Jubilee** (full quilt page 64). Whole or partial border print within central design

Examples of symmetrical and partially-symmetrical border-print fabrics; varying widths and scales of decorative designs that are printed parallel to the selvage edge, separated by much narrower strips of designs that are all related by color or one design printed over and over across the width of the fabric

Symmetrical

Partially symmetrical

One design printed over and over

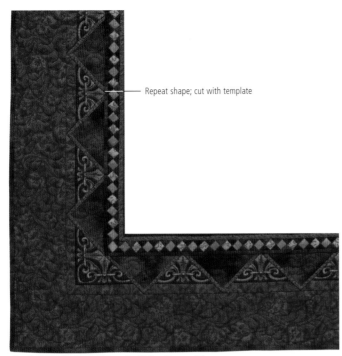

Repeat shape; cut with template

Detail of **Sophisticated Sampler** (full quilt page 13).

Repeat shape; cut with template

Detail of **My Journey** (full quilt page 71).

Detail of **Pinwheels** (full quilt page 71). Create your own border print by cutting varying widths of fabrics that are different in their visual texture such as stripes, florals, repeat motifs, and so on. Separate each with one or two very narrow (⅛'' or ¼'') borders of a very dark or hot color.

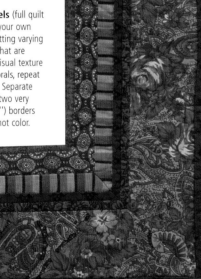

Detail of **Crossroad** (full quilt page 65). Use full or partial width of border print.

Detail of **Paws and Reflect** (full quilt page 70). Use to outline shapes or as a curved appliqué border (page 39).

However you choose to use border prints, you will find them to be a beautiful addition to your quilts. If this process is new to you, I encourage you to read through it carefully and then practice with paper and small dimensions to understand the concept before cutting up fabric.

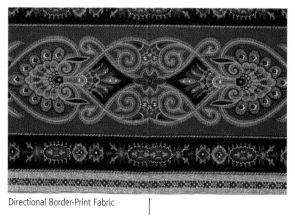

Directional Border-Print Fabric

Seam at center

Mirror-image corner using directional border print, seamed to change direction at the center of each side of the quilt.

Asymmetrical Border-Print Fabrics

Sawtooth Star, 1997, designed, machine pieced, and hand quilted by author. This quilt incorporates narrow and sawtooth borders in addition to a directional, asymmetrical border print. Asymmetrical border prints do not create mirror images at the corners. You can create four corners or opposite corners that are the same by positioning the same area of design at the center of each side but they will not be mirror images at the corner.

Cut and Sew Borders from a Symmetrical Border Print for a Square Quilt

1. Decide the total border width for your quilt.

2. Lay out your border-print fabric and choose the design area you want to use.

Use envelopes to section off the appropriate design areas.

3. Corner design possibilities are based on placing either the center of a motif or the area between motifs at the center of all four sides of the quilt.

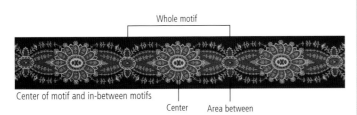

Center of motif and in-between motifs

Whole motif

Center   Area between

4. To see what the corner options would look like, measure out from the center of the chosen motif one half the total finished measurement of your quilt and place a mirror at a 45° angle at exactly that point to see how the corner would look. Do the same from the area between motifs and make your choice of corner designs.

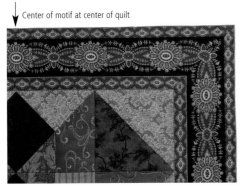

Center of motif at center of quilt

Corner options

Area between motifs at center of quilt

5. To cut the border strips, measure your quilt top (page 16). Add that number to the width of the border times two, plus 6" extra. This is generous and not exact. For example, if the quilt measures 60½" + 9" (2 x 4½"-wide border) + 6" extra = 75½" border strip length. Cut or tear a strip generously wider than the finished width plus seam allowance. If you tear the strips, allow at least ¾" extra on both long edges, which will be damaged and unusable. Additionally, I allow at least 1½" extra on the edge that will be bound (or finished if it is a final border) to ensure room to square up the quilt after it is quilted.

6. On one of the border strips, press and identify the exact area (on the edge that will be sewn to the quilt) that you want to see when your border is sewn. Place the ¼" ruler line on that area and trim off the excess, leaving an exact ¼" seam allowance beyond what you want to see. The opposite side requires no trimming until after the edge is finished. Do not get the two edges confused when sewing the borders to the quilt.

7. Working on the wrong side and the correct edge of one border length, place a pin at the exact center. Measure out from that pin one half the finished measurement of the quilt (30") and make a mark ¼" from the raw edge on the wrong side of the border print. Repeat in the opposite direction from the center pin. Repeat for the remaining three borders, being sure the markings are in exactly the same place on all four border strips to create perfectly matched corners.

30"   30"

Wrong side of border

8. Working on the wrong side of the quilt top, mark a dot at each corner ¼" from each raw edge. Also mark the center of each side of the quilt top.

Quilt, wrong side

9. Align the border onto the quilt top, right sides together. Match and pin the centers and corner dots. Be sure you are pinning the correct edge of the border print to the quilt top. It is important that the edges of both the border and quilt top be exactly even. Press and add pins between center and corners, then add more pins halfway between those, until you have adequately pinned for stable sewing.

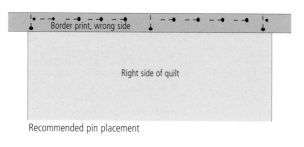

Border print, wrong side

Right side of quilt

Recommended pin placement

10. Lower your sewing machine needle right in front of the dot, take three small stitches forward and three backward, lengthen the stitch slightly and continue sewing across the quilt, sewing slowly and straight, removing pins as you approach them. When nearing the opposite corner, stop sewing, reduce the stitch length slightly, sew to just in front of the dot, backstitch three stitches and remove from the machine. Repeat for the remaining three borders. Press to set stitches, press seam allowance toward the borders, and examine carefully for accuracy before mitering the corners.

Cut and Sew Borders from a Symmetrical Border Print for a Rectangular Quilt

On rectangular quilts, it is unlikely you will be able to use the same motif or area between motifs at the center of all four sides to match the corners exactly, because you will be working with both length and width dimensions. You will need to seam the two side borders to create four perfectly matched corners. The seams will hardly be noticeable because you will be creating mirror images. You would notice if the corners were not matched.

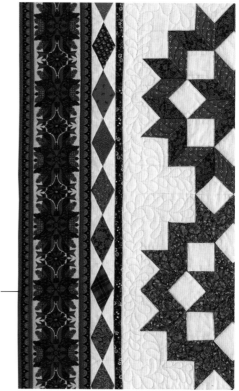

Seam

Detail of **Christmas Rose** (full quilt page 26). The seam is in the center of the side borders.

1. Measure your quilt (page 16). Let's say it's 60" x 70" finished.

2. Plan the corners and cut out only the top and bottom border strips as you did for a square quilt (page 29).

3. Place a pin at the center of the top border strip. Mark a dot one half the total finished width (30") in both directions as you did for a square quilt. Repeat for the bottom border.

4. Cut two more border strips for the sides being even more generous than the formula described in Step 5 on page 29.

5. Lay the top border, right-side up, on top of one of the side borders (also right-side up), toward one end, matching the fabric print exactly and allowing adequate mitering overlap. Place a dot on the side border in exactly the same place as it appears on the top border. Measure out from that dot half the finished length of the side of the quilt plus ¼" and cut (35¼"). You now have one half of one side border which serves as the template for cutting three more. Take this half side border you have just cut and place it at the other end of the same side border you have been working on. Place it face down or right sides together, which creates its mirror image, matching the fabric design exactly. Make a miter dot on the side border edge exactly where it is on the template. Measure out 35¼" from the dot and cut. Repeat this process again for the remaining side border.

6. Sew two appropriate halves together to create the two side borders. Press the seams open.

7. Sew all four borders to your quilt top and miter the corners.

Forming Mitered Corners by Hand

To create a flat, smooth miter, you must stop sewing ¼" from the corner and backstitch when adding the borders to the quilt top.

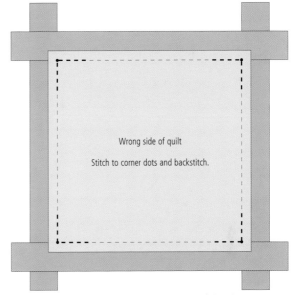

Wrong side of quilt

Stitch to corner dots and backstitch.

Extend both borders out straight, one on top of the other.

Position your quilt right-side up and work with one corner at a time on the ironing board or a flat surface. Be sure the quilt is supported and not hanging off the surface.

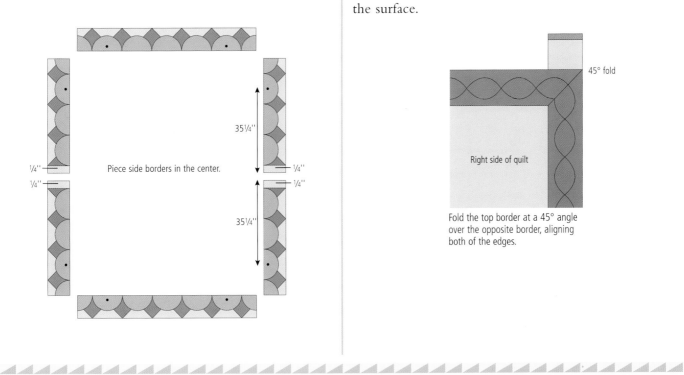

35¼"

¼" ¼"

¼" ¼"

Piece side borders in the center.

35¼"

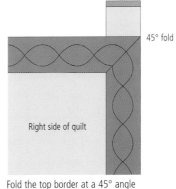

45° fold

Right side of quilt

Fold the top border at a 45° angle over the opposite border, aligning both of the edges.

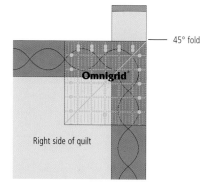

45° fold

Right side of quilt

Align the mitered fold on each corner with the 45° line on a large square ruler. The border edges should align with the outside edges of the ruler. Press, pin, then baste the miter fold in place.

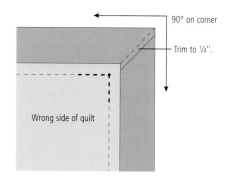

90° on corner

Trim to ¼''.

Wrong side of quilt

Trim excess to ¼'' seam allowance and hand appliqué the miter closed using matching thread color and very tiny stitches.

Noteworthy

If you want to miter corners and the widths of the borders are not the same, stop stitching, and backstitch ¼'' from the corner in both directions. Once the borders are sewn on, press them out flat and looking from the right side, fold the top border under until the outer edge of both borders meet at the corners. Use a square ruler to ensure a 90° corner. Press, pin, baste, and hand stitch the miter seam closed. The angle of the miter will not be 45° but the corner will be 90°.

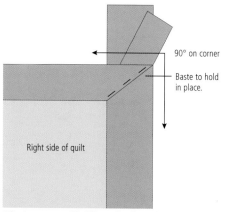

90° on corner

Baste to hold in place.

Right side of quilt

Mitering corner with different border widths

Forming Mitered Corners by Machine

Focus on one corner at a time and work from the wrong side of the quilt. Extend both borders out straight and flat, one over the other. To assure a 90° corner and a 45° miter:

1. Place a square ruler over the corner and align the 45° line of the ruler over both the outer corner crevice where the two borders overlap and the ¼'' miter dot. The outer edges of both borders should align with the outside edges of the square ruler.
2. Draw a straight line from the crevice to the miter dot.

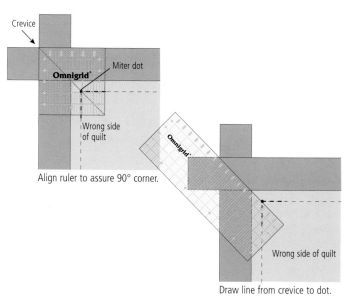

Crevice

Miter dot

Wrong side of quilt

Align ruler to assure 90° corner.

Wrong side of quilt

Draw line from crevice to dot.

3. Reverse the borders' position and repeat Steps 1 and 2 to mark the other border.
4. Position the two borders right sides together, matching and pinning their ¼'' dots and drawn lines exactly. Sew on the drawn line, beginning at the outside corner edge to the ¼'' dot, backstitching at both ends.
5. Trim excess to ¼'' seam allowance and press to one side.

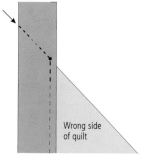

Wrong side of quilt

Sew on line from outer edge to dot, backstitching at both ends.

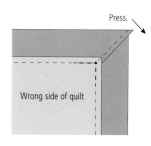

Press.

Wrong side of quilt

APPLIQUÉ BORDERS

The following will explain how I design, fit, mark, and construct a continuous, curved line. It might serve as a foundation for vines and shapes to be appliquéd onto, curved appliqué borders, swags, curved borders taken from border prints, and edge-finish shapes.

Continuous, Symmetrical Curved Line

Various shapes (leaves, flowers, etc.) can be appliquéd to a continuous, symmetrical curved line (tight, close curve, or longer, spread out curve) that undulates around your quilt. This can also be an edge-finished shape. Both are made up of a single shape that is repeated around the quilt. To create this curved line:

1. Sketch a design.
2. Divide the finished length(s) of your border (minus the corner space) into equal repeat spaces.
3. Draw a curve that reflects your design and fits into a single repeat space.
4. Plan a pleasing corner design.

Dividing the finished length of the border to establish a repeat unit length can be done in three ways.

1. Work with a scale drawing on graph paper. Place two mirrors taped at a 90° angle onto the dotted lines on the illustration. You will see the whole quilt with four options. The repeat unit needs space at each of the border edges (½" to 1" on each side) unless it is designed as an edge finish.

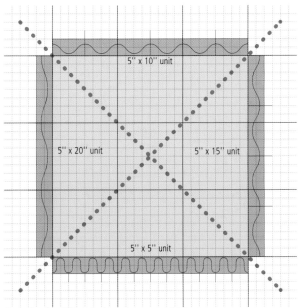

5" x 10" unit

5" x 20" unit   5" x 15" unit

5" x 5" unit

Scale drawing, 60" quilt, 1 graph square = 2½"

2. Cut a piece of calculator or other roll paper the finished length of your border, minus the corners. The width is not relevant at the moment. Fold the strip of paper in half lengthwise, continuing to fold in half accordion style (fold each half back and forth on itself), until you find the proportion appropriate for your sketch or design. If your quilt is longer than 60", you can work with half the length of your border.

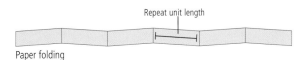

Repeat unit length

Paper folding

3. Using a calculator to find the length of the repeat unit, divide the finished length of the border by an estimated number of repeats until you arrive at a number that divides equally, is proportionate, and reflects your design. Because appliqué is more forgiving than piecing, you can also increase or decrease the length of the unit in the center of the border to accommodate a slight discrepancy or left-over space. This applies to edge-finish shapes as well. A quick way to *estimate* the length of the repeat unit is to double the width of the border.

Noteworthy

If the quilt is a rectangle, you will be working with two different border measurements. In the division process, if the repeat units are not exactly the same but close, you can use both repeat lengths. You could also add a spacer border to bring the sides up to a size that allows the same repeat length unit for all borders. Details concerning spacer borders are on page 24.

Once you have determined the length of the repeat unit, decide on the width of your border, keeping in mind proportion and scale.

Once you have determined the length and width of your repeat unit, cut two or three rectangles from graph or tracing paper the exact finished size (cutting more than one allows the opportunity for a variety of design comparisons).

1. Sharply fold the rectangle into quarters both vertically and horizontally to create a grid.

2. Fold the rectangle in half vertically and, referring to your scale drawing, lightly draw the curve, then darken it. Turn the paper over, leaving it folded and trace the line on the other half. Open the paper and you have the two far ends (half) of your complete repeat-unit design.

3. Re-fold the sides into the center vertically, then fold in half horizontally, trace the curve. Open the paper and you now you have a complete symmetrical curve for a repeat unit.

A mirror positioned at one short edge lets you see two whole repeats to get an idea of size, flow, and proportion. You might also sketch some shapes on it (leaves or flowers) to get a feel for the border. Do several different drawings to compare and then choose the best one for your quilt.

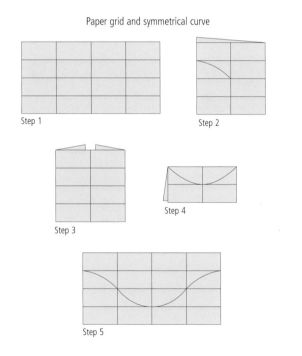

Paper grid and symmetrical curve

Step 1

Step 2

Step 3

Step 4

Step 5

To create an interwoven, continuous curved line, after you have created a symmetrical curve as described above, fold the paper rectangle repeat unit in half horizontally, retrace the curves, turn it over, and retrace the curves again.

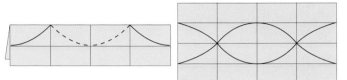

Paper grid, interwoven design

Corners

Now you need to connect the two sides by designing a corner. Create a variety of corner designs so you have options. Notice in the examples that if the ends of the repeat shape end low, near the seam, you can create a loop in the corner or a narrow curved corner. If the ends of the repeat shape end high, near the outer edge, you can create a more full, round-shaped corner. You must decide that before making the template. Once you have decided on a corner design, draw it actual size on a square of paper the size of the width of the border plus ½" for seam allowance.

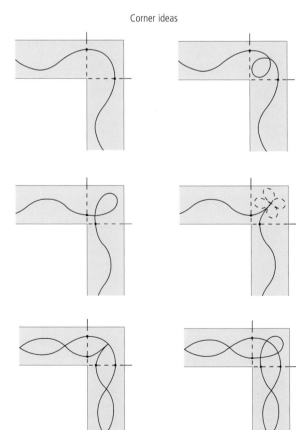

Corner ideas

1. To mark the symmetrical curved line you have designed on unattached borders, first make a plastic template, from the paper drawing, adding ¼" seam allowance to the long flat edge only and identify the center of the shape.

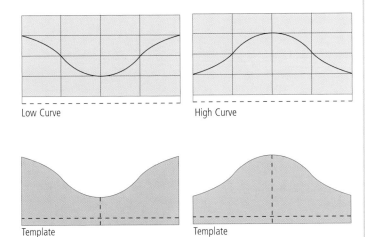

Low Curve   High Curve

Template   Template

2. On the right side of the fabric border strip, mark ¼" in from each end and the center. This allows for seam allowance and identifies where you will begin and end the design.

3. Place the template on one end of the border at the ¼" mark, tracing the curve and marking the beginning and center of each repeat shape in the seam allowance. These markings will help make any adjustments at the center area, by lengthening or shortening the center curve. Work from both ends toward the center.

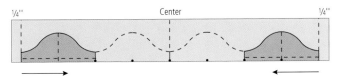

¼"   Center   ¼"

Trace curve onto border with template.

Appliqué the design. Repeat for the remaining three borders. Sew the side borders onto the quilt. Add two corner squares to each end of the top and bottom borders and add the borders to the quilt. Mark the curved line

around the corner by placing the actual-size drawing under each fabric corner and trace. Appliqué the corner area to complete the design. *Skating by Snowlight* on page 73 is a wonderful example of continuous, symmetrical curved line use for appliqué.

Symmetrical and Asymmetrical Curved-Edge

This style of border can be created from a repeat symmetrical or asymmetrical curve. The curved border is then basted and appliquéd onto an existing mitered border already sewn to the quilt. The existing border underneath the appliquéd border will be trimmed away. A symmetrical curved border is designed by developing a repeat-unit length in the same way as a continuous curved line was designed, as described earlier.

Passion Flower, 1999, designed, machine pieced, and hand quilted by author. This quilt uses both swags and a symmetrical curved appliqué border to soften and enhance the geometrical piecing of the blocks.

O' Christmas Tree, 1993, designed, machine pieced, and hand quilted by author. This quilt has an asymmetrical curved appliqué border.

1. To design an asymmetrical curved border edge, decide the width first, then sketch on paper to create a free-form, pleasing shape to travel around the quilt taking corners into account. Folding a square or rectangle of paper into quarters and scissor cutting the edges can also be a springboard for ideas, especially if you use mirrors to see a whole design. This does not need to be actual size, because you are just designing and gathering ideas.

Scissor cutting a folded paper square and rectangle

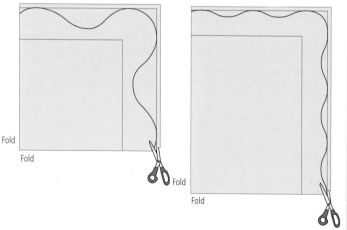

2. On a square quilt, you only need to design from the center of one side to the corner (one eighth of the whole), then view the design with mirrors.

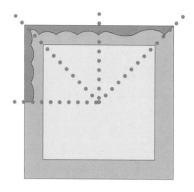

Place mirrors on dotted lines. Darkest shaded area indicates appliqué border.

3. On a rectangular quilt you must design from the center of one short border, around the corner to the center of the longer border. Again, place mirrors appropriately to see the whole design.

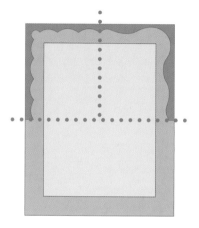

This asymmetrical curved line could also be marked onto a border and used as a vine placement for appliquéing shapes onto, or used as an edge-finish shape.

4. Once you decide on a design shape, make an exact, actual-size template by drawing your sketched shape on graph paper to scale. If you are using a symmetrical, repeat shape, trace it onto the graph paper working from the corner to the center, adding ¼" to the outer straight edge.

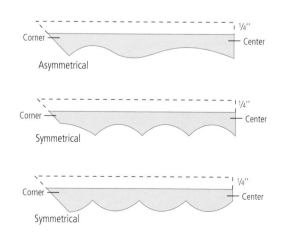

5. Cut out this shape from the graph paper exactly on the line. This is your template. It should lay perfectly on the existing mitered border it will be appliquéd onto, from the corner miter to the middle of one side. For a rectangular quilt, you will have two templates, one for half of the shorter side and one for half of the longer side.

Cut four lengthwise grain strips of fabric, twice the length of the template plus 8" for insurance and 1" wider than the template. Fold this border strip in half to identify the center, and place a pin or mark a centerline. Lay the graph paper template onto the right side of one border strip, matching the center of the fabric border strip to the short straight edge of the paper design and the raw edge of the fabric to the long straight edge of the template. To prevent the paper from moving while marking, fold or roll small pieces of drafting or painter's tape, sticky side out to have double-stick capability, at various places for stability. Carefully trace the exact curved shape onto the fabric border, stopping at the miter. Do not trace the miter angle. Repeat this on the remaining three borders for a square quilt and on one remaining border for a rectangular quilt. Remove the paper template and the tape, flip the paper template over, reapply the tape to the other side of the paper template aligning the paper from the center to the opposite end, and trace again, completing all borders.

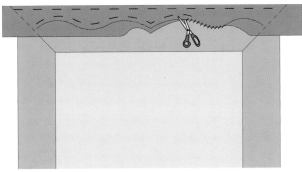

Flip at center

Template

Trace curved shape onto border.

6. Position one curved border onto the appropriate existing border, right-side up, aligning the outer edge and matching the centers of the border strip and quilt exactly. Pin, then baste in place ¼" from both the outer straight edge and curved design line. Begin trimming the excess about 2"–3" away from the miter angle and ³⁄₁₆" from the curved line for the seam allowance. Remove basting as necessary and needle-turn appliqué the ³⁄₁₆" seam allowance under, stopping 2"–3" from the opposite miter angle. Repeat for the remaining three borders.

Corners

Form and miter the corners by hand (page 31). Trim away the excess and continue appliquéing the curved corner. When appliquéing the miter closed, sew only the curved border fabrics together so the existing border underneath is free and unattached. When all corners are formed and appliquéd, remove the remaining basting, turn the quilt top to the back and trim away the existing, mitered border ¼" from the appliqué stitches.

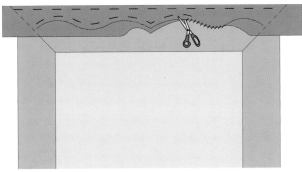

Begin trimming and needle-turn appliqué.

Appliquéd asymmetrical border

Swags

A swag border can be simple in shape and use only one fabric or be more complex in shape and use multiple fabrics.

Swag styles

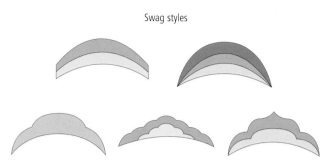

Think about how the corner might turn, how wide or narrow the connection between swags will be, where the swag will rest within the total width of the border, and also whether there will be a separate appliqué design over the connection area.

Connections

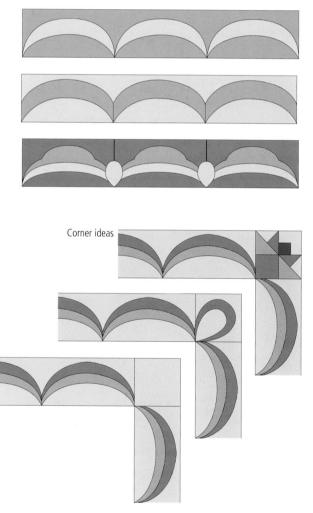

Corner ideas

Drawing Swags

1. To create a proportionate swag shape, first create a paper repeat-length unit as described earlier for a Continuous, Symmetrical Curved Line on page 33. This unit is the length and width of the swag only, not necessarily the width of the border. Fold the paper unit into quarters vertically and horizontally, to create a grid. Open the paper and fold it in half vertically as described on page 34.

2. Referring to the illustration, draw one half of the swag shape. The distance between A and B is the width of the connection from one swag to another. It can be as wide as you choose. The distance between C and D is how deep or high the swag will be.

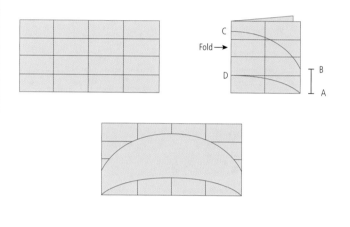

3. Connect A to D and B to C to form one half of the swag shape. You could also connect A to C if you do not want a wide connection. *Shadow Baskets* on page 72 uses a simple swag style. Turn the folded paper over and trace the curved lines on the other side to complete the swag shape. If you are working on a rectangular quilt and need two slightly different sizes of swags, keep the height and connection the same and increase or decrease the length of the swag only. Once you have a basic size and shape, you can add details.

Marking Swags on Border

1. To mark the swag placement on the border, first sew the borders and corners to the quilt.

2. Make a template from your drawing of the swag shape and corner shape, do not add any seam allowance and be very exact. Identify the center of each swag.

3. Identify the center of each border. Using the template and working from each end towards the middle, lightly mark (with a removable marking tool), the beginning and ending of each swag to be sure your size and placement fit exactly as planned in your sketch.

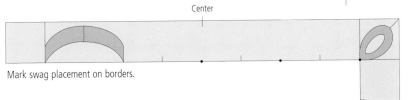
Mark swag placement on borders.

4. Working on one border at a time, create the swag shapes from fabric and appliqué in place.
5. Create and appliqué the corner shapes in place last.

Border-Print Appliqué Borders

A border-print fabric that has a clearly defined curved-edge design works best. Look for an edge that is appealing, feasible to appliqué, and symmetrical, to easily create four corners the same. See Border-Print Fabric Borders beginning on page 26. Carefully examine the border prints you have, remembering you can always make adjustments or simplify the curved edge if necessary. The design rewards are high with this technique because you benefit from the beautiful print of the border fabric, the shape the cut edge creates when appliquéd, and the color and print of the backdrop border you appliqué onto. *Paws and Reflect* on page 70 uses this technique. Once the border print is appliquéd onto the four backdrop fabric borders, you will proceed the same as you would for any mitered border-print border, matching the corner design exactly.

1. Determine the exact finished area you want to expose. Cut ¼" from the straight edge that will be machine sewn to your quilt and cut approximately ³⁄₁₆" from the finished curved edge to be appliquéd.
2. Cut the four backdrop-fabric borders the length necessary for mitering and the width desired. Align the straight edge of the border print to one edge of the backdrop border, both right-side up, being mindful of centers and corners for mitering as discussed on page 31, Border-Print Borders. Baste, then appliqué, the border print to the backdrop borders.
3. Needle-turn the ³⁄₁₆" seam allowance under at the curved edge. Repeat for the remaining three borders.
4. Remove the basting and cut away the border underneath the border print to within ¼" of the appliqué stitches.
5. Sew the borders to the quilt top, placing the border-print design appropriately to create matched corners, starting and stopping ¼" from the corner, and backstitching at both ends. Miter the corners as discussed on page 31, Forming Mitered Corners by Hand.

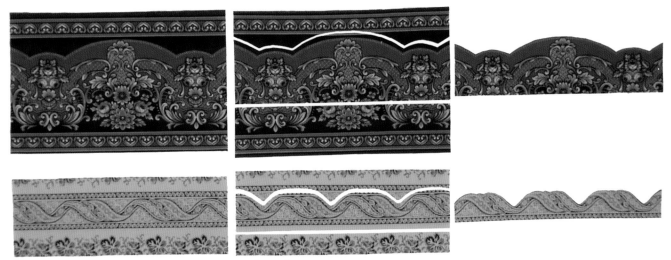
Border Print Candidates. Cut curved edge of border print with a ³⁄₁₆" seam allowance.

CORNER TRIANGLE BORDERS

This style of border takes a square block or design and, by turning it on point and adding a triangle on each edge of the square, creates a significantly larger quilt and the potential to transform it into a more elegant design. The area within the triangles can be pieced, appliquéd, or left plain for quilting. Use a border print or any combination of these. See *Crossroad* on page 65.

Corner triangle borders

These corner triangle border areas can also reflect one quarter of the center design as shown in *Paws and Reflect* on page 70. Be sure to do a scale drawing to proportionately size your shapes and position them relative to the central design.

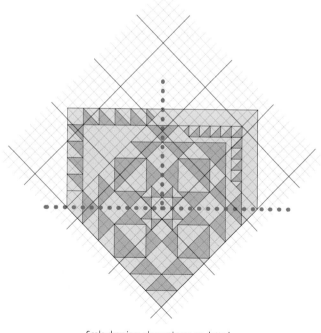

Scale drawing; place mirrors on dotted lines to see whole design two ways.

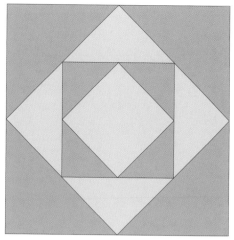

Add multiple rounds of corner triangles to the square on point.

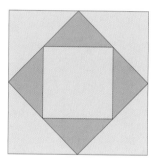

In some instances the central design or block must be kept on square (a house block). In that case, you can add triangles to bring it to a square on point, then add four more triangles to bring it back to square.

Sizing Corner Triangles

The corner triangles are one quarter of the finished size of the central design or block.

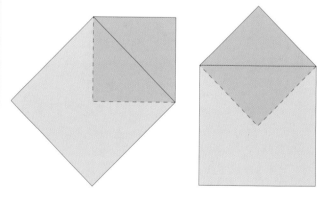

To figure out the finished size of the triangles you divide the finished size of the square by 1.414 (for a more detailed explanation of this number, refer to Diagonal Measurements on page 60). Because the answer will be in tenths on a calculator, refer to Decimal Equivalents (page 62) to round off to a ruler-friendly number for rotary cutting or make a template. If you are cutting these triangles from plain fabric you will add ⅞" to the answer and cut two squares that size, cut them in half diagonally and sew them to the four sides of your block. Cutting this way keeps the straight of grain on the two short sides of the triangle and the outer edge of the quilt. For example, if your center design is 24" finished, you would divide; 24" ÷ 1.414 = 16.973 = 17" (finished) + ⅞" = 17⅞". Cut two squares that size, then cut in half diagonally.

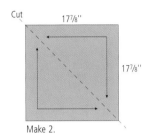

If you are designing within the triangle area, draw the size of the finished triangle on graph paper and using your scale drawing as a map, develop the design in actual size. Once you have actualized the design shapes in the triangle, add ¼" seam allowance to all sides of each shape, if rotary cutting. If the sizes of the shapes are not ruler-friendly, make templates.

Simply speaking, place the pieced, appliqué, or border-print designs wherever you choose within the triangle space and fill in the remaining space with fabric strips or other shapes.

Additional Opportunities

Border opportunities are also exposed whenever you have multiple or repeat blocks that are placed on point because you will have both corner (one quarter the block size) and side (one half the block size) triangles that square off the design. When this occurs, you can fracture the space to create a design and begin the border process.

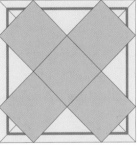

Flamenco, 2000, designed, machine pieced, and machine quilted by author. This quilt combines geometric and curved patchwork with corner triangles, narrow borders, a border print, and a plain fabric border. The curved and piped edge finish bring this quilt to a beautiful conclusion.

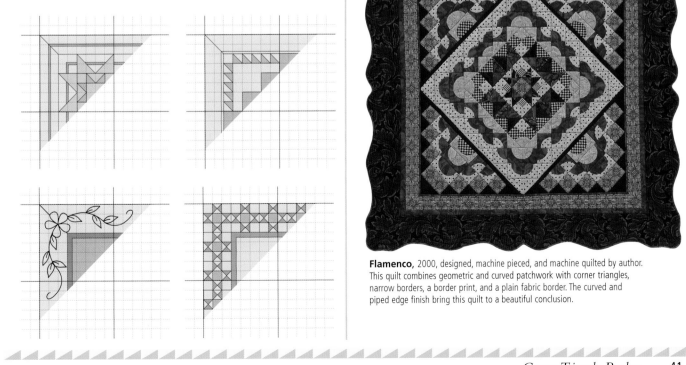

PIECED BORDERS

A pieced border is a series of patchwork or geometric shapes (repeat units) that relate to the central design and are joined together to form a continuous length that most often travels around the outside edge of the quilt.

There are multitudes of pieced border styles and variations derived from a few basic groups commonly used in traditional-style quilts, such as checkerboards, sawtooth, flying geese, diamonds, repeat blocks, chain of squares, parallelograms, and dogtooth.

You can fracture the space within a repeat unit any way you choose. Never sacrifice design for ruler-friendly numbers; simply make templates.

Checkerboard

Description

This non-directional style of border most often consists of squares, although rectangles can be used in concert with squares or alone.

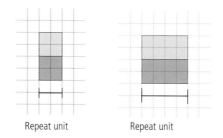

Repeat unit   Repeat unit

They add interest to many quilt designs, including those not incorporating a checkerboard in the central design and can also be used as a filler. *Crossroad* on page 65 and *Epicenter* on page 75 are good examples.

Color

Any two highly-contrasting values of one or more colors give a dramatic, choppy effect. If the values of the colors used are gradated (moving from light to dark in sequence), movement or shimmer is created.

Cutting, Piecing, Pressing

Cut the strips (on the lengthwise grain if possible), the desired finished size of one square, plus ½" for seam allowance. Join the strips and press the seam to the darker fabric to create opposing seams when assembling. If the checkerboards are ¼" to 1", open and trim the seams.

Segments from the strip units are cut the same dimension as the cut strips. For example, if the checkerboard strips are cut 1½" wide, the segments cut from the strip unit are cut 1½" wide (1" finished).

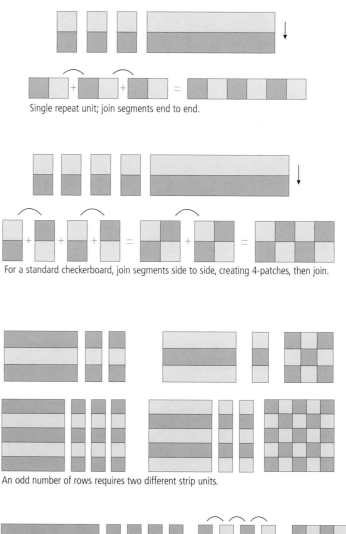

Single repeat unit; join segments end to end.

For a standard checkerboard, join segments side to side, creating 4-patches, then join.

An odd number of rows requires two different strip units.

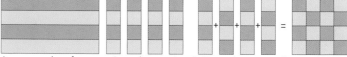

An even number of rows requires only one strip unit. Every other segment is rotated 180°.

Rectangles are often twice as long as they are wide.

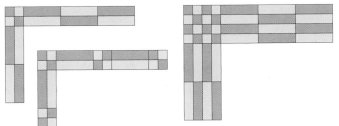

Rectangles can be used alone or with squares.

Corners

Corner considerations are dependent upon whether you have an even or odd number of repeats per side of the quilt and how many colors make up the checkerboard.

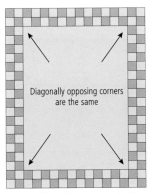

Even number of repeats on all sides, square or rectangle

Odd number of repeats on top and bottom, even number of repeats on the sides, rectangle

Odd number of repeats on all sides, square or rectangle

Variations

Variations can be created by changing the scale of the checkerboard. You can either double or half the repeat unit length.

Samples

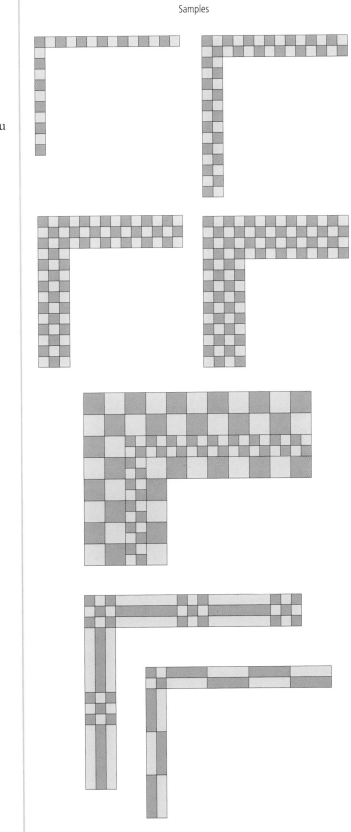

Sawtooth

Description

This directional style of border is very versatile, and enhances most traditional designs, whether or not they include triangles. See *Sedona* page 6.

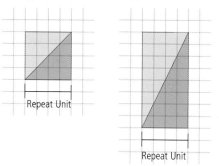

Repeat Unit

Repeat Unit

Color

Sawtooth borders are often created from two colors or fabrics. The value contrast can be high or subtle, depending upon the effect desired. Scrap borders are also effective. Refer to Planned Random on page 12.

Cutting, Piecing, Pressing

To cut individual sawtooth triangles that include ¼" seam allowance on all sides, cut squares the finished size of the repeat unit plus, ⅞". Then cut the square in half diagonally. Press the seam allowance toward the darker color. If you are making small sawteeth (¼" to 1") press open and trim the seam.

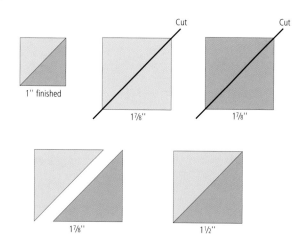

Cut

Cut

1" finished

1⅞"

1⅞"

1⅞"

1½"

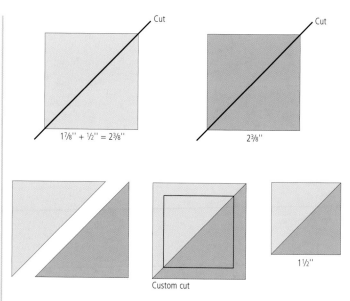

Cut

Cut

1⅞" + ½" = 2⅜"

2⅜"

Custom cut

1½"

Oversize, then trim to size.

To cut sawtooth rectangle repeat units that are twice as high as they are wide, add 1⁵⁄₁₆" to the finished height of the rectangle and 1¹⁄₁₆" to the finished width. A 2" x 4" finished half-rectangle repeat unit would be cut 2¹¹⁄₁₆" x 5⁵⁄₁₆", then cut in half diagonally. To create mirror-image triangles, which change their direction, cut in the opposite direction.

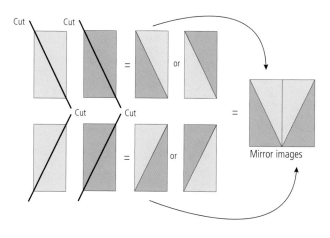

Cut

Cut

=

or

Cut

Cut

=

or

=

Mirror images

Mark a dot at each end of the long side, ¼" from the edge of each triangle, on the wrong side. Align the triangles right sides together, pin at the dots, and sew from edge to edge. Press the seam allowance to the darker color or open and trim if making small units.

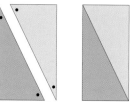

Mark dots, align, pin, sew, and press.

Another cutting option would be to draw the finished rectangle on graph paper, draw a diagonal line from corner to corner, add ¼" seam allowance on all four sides and make a rectangle template. Then make an oversized unit as described on page 44 for square sawtooth repeat units and custom cut the exact size you want using the template. You could also make a triangle template that includes the ¼" seam allowance and cut individual triangles to then sew together.

Corners

Because sawtooth borders are asymmetrical and directional, when they are positioned to travel around the quilt with an even or odd number of repeat units, clockwise or counterclockwise, inconsistent corners are created.

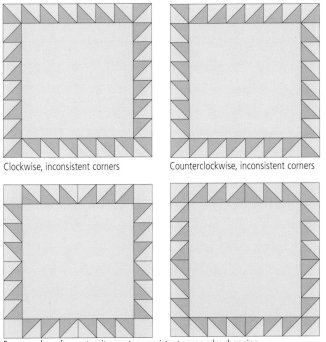

Clockwise, inconsistent corners   Counterclockwise, inconsistent corners

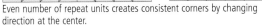

Even number of repeat units creates consistent corners by changing direction at the center.

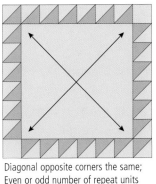

Diagonal opposite corners the same;
Even or odd number of repeat units

If you want to change an odd number of repeats to an even number on all sides of the quilt or perhaps on only two sides, refer to page 24, Spacer Borders. The corners can be a plain square or a sawtooth repeat unit.

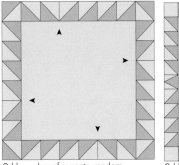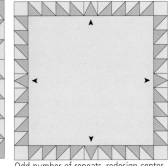

Odd number of repeats, random direction change, corners consistent   Odd number of repeats, redesign center unit, corners consistent

Odd number of repeats, redesign center three units, corners consistent

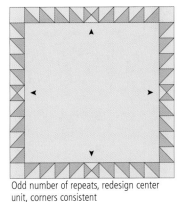

Odd number of repeats, redesign center unit, corners consistent

Changing direction on a rectangular sawtooth border would be the same as the square sawtooth border. The corners are automatically consistent because they are usually plain squares the size of the height of the repeat unit.

Variations

Variations can easily be created by sewing multiple rows of sawteeth of the same size and scale, as seen in *Five-Patch Sampler* on page 7, or varying the scale as seen in *Starry Night* on page 10. You can also mix square and rectangular sawteeth or place the rectanglar sawteeth on their long edge to create another variation. Additionally, you can fracture one of the triangles in the repeat unit into multiple triangles as seen in *Baskets* on page 73.

Shaded sawtooth border is another variation and is created from three triangles, two are quarter-square triangles with the straight grain on the long side of the triangle and one is a half-square triangle with the straight of grain on the two short sides of the triangle.

To cut the two smaller quarter-square triangles and keep the straight of grain on the outside edge of the unit and include the ¼" seam allowance on all sides, cut squares of appropriate fabric the finished size of the unit plus 1¼", then cut into quarters diagonally.

Join two small triangles, finger-press toward the darker color, and join to the larger triangle (which is cut by adding ⅞" to the finished size of the repeat unit as described earlier) to complete the repeat unit. Press this seam open. The repeat unit should now measure 1½" square. Again, I would oversize and custom cut this unit for accuracy. Examples of a shaded sawtooth border are *Medallion Sampler* on page 71 which changes direction at the center and *Floral Fantasy* on page 73, which changes direction randomly.

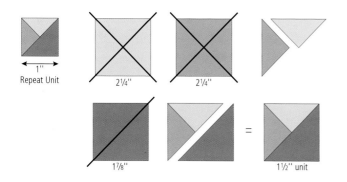

Corners and changing direction are the same as described on page 45.

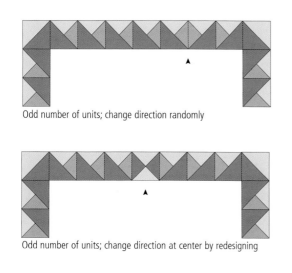

Odd number of units; change direction randomly

Odd number of units; change direction at center by redesigning

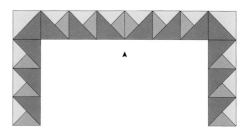

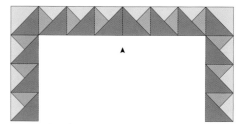

Even number of units; change direction at center

Samples

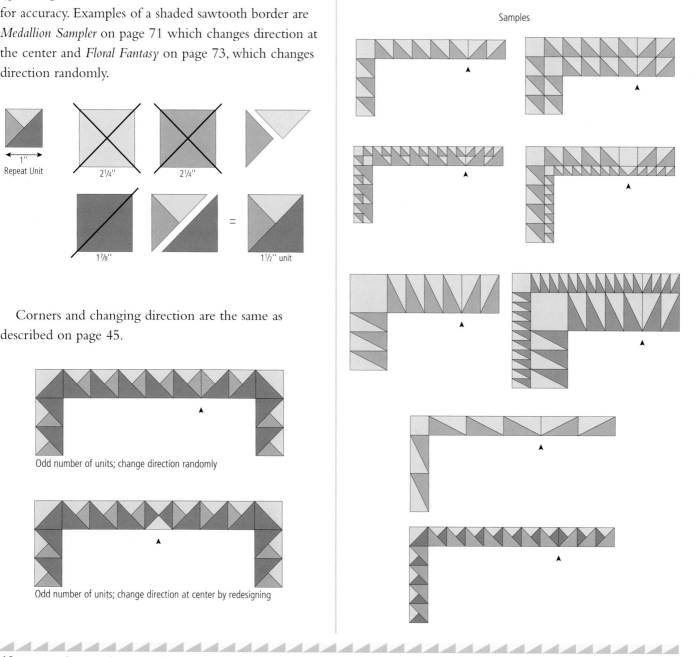

Flying Geese

Description

This style of border is directional, rectangular, and traditionally twice as high as it is wide. It consists of three right triangles. The two smaller triangles are each half the size of the larger center triangle.

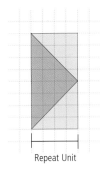

Repeat Unit

Color

This border repeat unit is most often colored so that the larger triangle holds the color and the two smaller triangles are background or are the same value as what they touch to camouflage the seam and allow the "geese" to fly. This, of course, could be reversed or you could have the small triangles each be a different color. All the large triangles ("geese") could be one color or a sampling of colors that are in the central design. A gradation of one or more colors is also an effective option. *Rhapsody in Bloom* on page 72 and *Desert Stars* on page 77 are examples of this style of border and each incorporates a different corner option.

Cutting, Piecing, Pressing

METHOD 1: INDIVIDUAL TRIANGLES

For Shape A, add 1¼" to the finished height of the unit. If your repeat unit is 2" x 4" finished, (4" + 1¼" = 5¼") cut a 5¼" square. Cut into quarters diagonally (4 Shape A triangles).

For Shape B, add ⅞" to the finished length of the unit (2" + ⅞" = 2⅞"). Cut a 2⅞" square and cut in half diagonally (2 Shape B triangles).

Join 1 Shape B to 1 Shape A, press toward Shape B. Add the remaining Shape B and press.

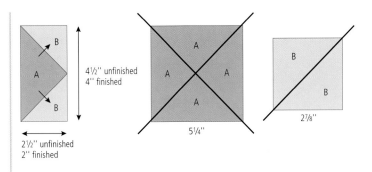

4½" unfinished / 4" finished

2½" unfinished / 2" finished

5¼"

2⅞"

METHOD 2: DOUBLE HALF-SQUARE TRIANGLES

This unit can also be created with a rectangle and two squares. Making the same size unit as described for individual triangles, add ½" to both the finished length and width of the unit (2½" x 4½") and cut a rectangle for Shape A. Add ½" to the finished length of the unit (2½") and cut two squares for Shape B. Draw a diagonal line on the wrong side of each square. Align the shapes, sew on the line, trim, and press.

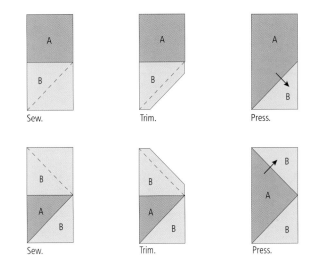

Sew. — Trim. — Press.

Sew. — Trim. — Press.

When joining repeat units, press seam allowances away from the points.

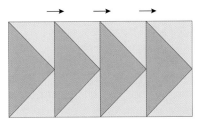

Corners

There are several possibilities for geese orientation to create corners that are all the same. You can change from an odd to an even number of repeat units on two or all sides by adding spacer borders page 24.

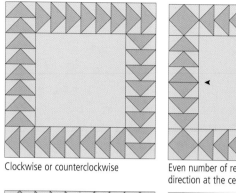

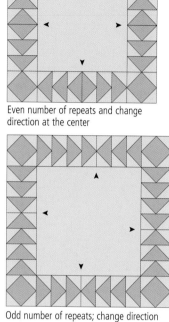

Clockwise or counterclockwise

Even number of repeats and change direction at the center

Even number of repeats; change direction at the center

Odd number of repeats; change direction randomly

Samples

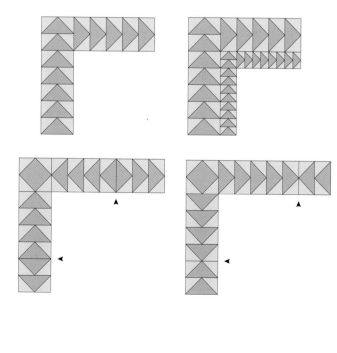

Woven Strips

This style of border has a floating quality and the primary design originates in and flows from the corners. It is created on a grid from the corner and extends outward into the side borders. The side border extensions can meet and be continuous or be separated.

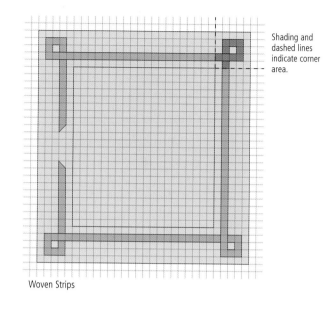

Shading and dashed lines indicate corner area.

Woven Strips

Begin designing by sketching ribbons intertwining. Transfer the rough sketch to graph paper, straightening the curved lines. Triangles can also be used—the ideas are endless.

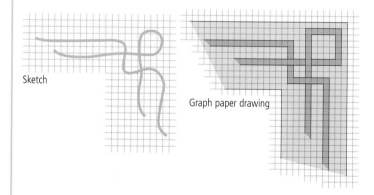

Sketch

Graph paper drawing

The corner design determines the width of the borders. Decide whether the strips will be positioned on the top and bottom edge of the border or will float within the border space. Follow the established scale drawing for cutting and piecing, always determining the finished shape or width of strips and then adding ½" for seam allowance. *Gizmo* on page 76 is one example of this style of border.

Color

Using colored pencils, explore the many color and fabric opportunities to make the strips weave over and under each other. The background in this style of border is important to clarify the corner design and is a perfect place for quilting.

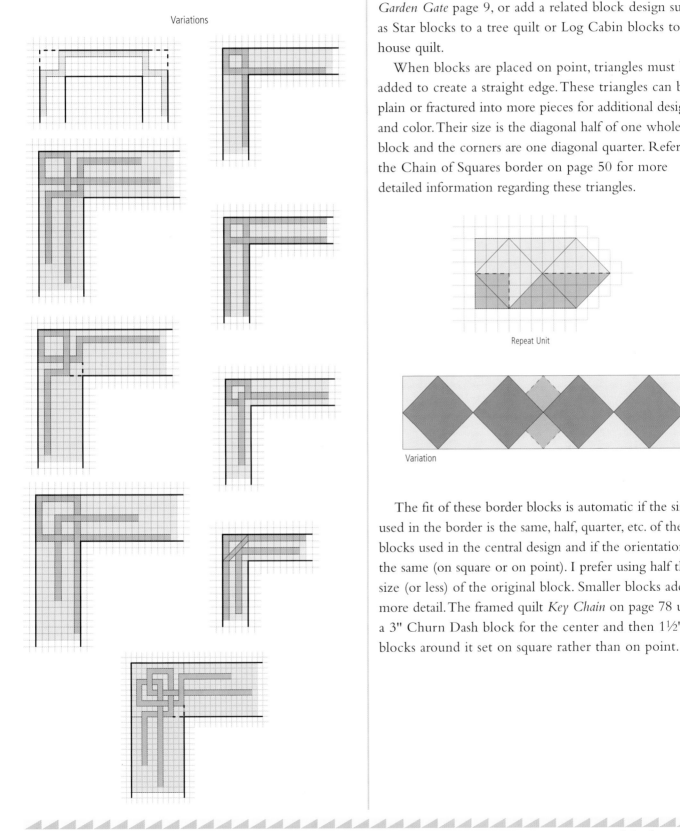

Variations

Repeat Blocks

Description

This non-directional style of border uses whole blocks and can be a way to dress up a simple design or add detail to an already beautiful quilt. You could repeat blocks that already exist in the central design of the quilt as I did in *Garden Gate* page 9, or add a related block design such as Star blocks to a tree quilt or Log Cabin blocks to a house quilt.

When blocks are placed on point, triangles must be added to create a straight edge. These triangles can be plain or fractured into more pieces for additional design and color. Their size is the diagonal half of one whole block and the corners are one diagonal quarter. Refer to the Chain of Squares border on page 50 for more detailed information regarding these triangles.

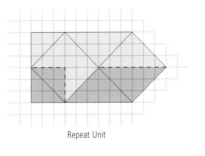

Repeat Unit

Variation

The fit of these border blocks is automatic if the size used in the border is the same, half, quarter, etc. of the blocks used in the central design and if the orientation is the same (on square or on point). I prefer using half the size (or less) of the original block. Smaller blocks add more detail. The framed quilt *Key Chain* on page 78 uses a 3" Churn Dash block for the center and then 1½" blocks around it set on square rather than on point.

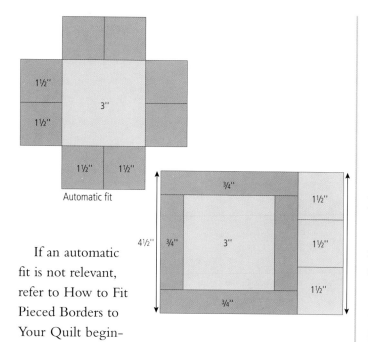

Automatic fit

If an automatic fit is not relevant, refer to How to Fit Pieced Borders to Your Quilt beginning on page 57. When adding blocks that are placed on point, the repeat unit size is the diagonal measurement from point to point. See Diagonal Measurements on page 60. *Desert Stars* on page 77 incorporates on-point blocks in the border that are not an automatic fit and required the Checkerboard border as a spacer border (page 24) to accommodate the size of the blocks in the border. You can also separate blocks in the border with sashing for design or spacing purposes or for creating more ruler-friendly numbers to work with; see *Star of Bethlehem* page 78.

Samples

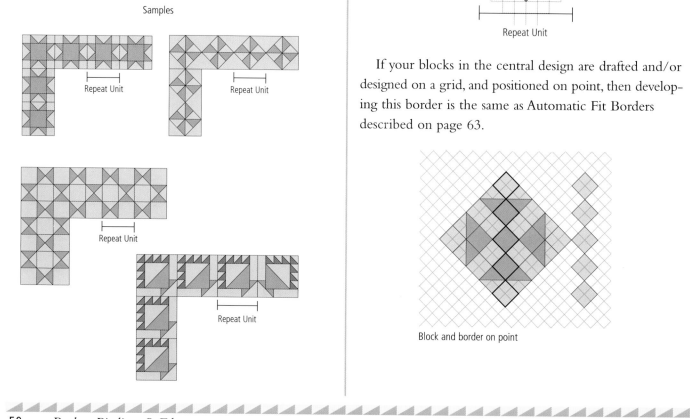

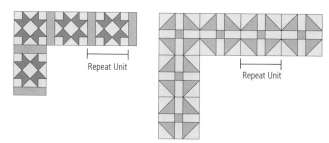

Chain of Squares

Description

This non-directional border consists of a single or multiple rows of squares placed on point with triangles that fill in the edge to create a straight border.

> ## Noteworthy
>
> Because this border places the squares on point, it is very important that you have a clear understanding of Diagonal Measurements beginning on page 60.

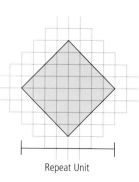

Repeat Unit

If your blocks in the central design are drafted and/or designed on a grid, and positioned on point, then developing this border is the same as Automatic Fit Borders described on page 63.

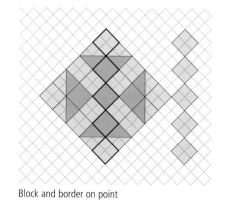

Block and border on point

Color

The squares can be all one color as seen in the *Diamond Jubilee* detail, on page 26, or two colors as in *Sophisticated Sampler* detail, on page 12, or a variety of colors as seen in *Star Crossed*, on page 72. There might also be times when you want to custom-cut a particular motif from a fabric. In that case, make a template for the square shape as seen in *Twilight* on page 76. The edge triangles can be the same color or different. If you match the value of the edge triangles to the fabric they touch, the seamline will be camouflaged and the squares will seem to float. You can also custom-cut the triangle shape repeatedly from a border-print fabric to add further detail, as seen in *My Journey* on page 27.

Cutting, Piecing, Pressing

If the blocks in the quilt are positioned on point, cut the squares for the border the established grid dimension of the block, plus seam allowance. For example, if the grid dimension of the blocks is 2½", cut 3" squares for the Chain of Squares border and position them on point as well.

The size of the edge triangles is the diagonal half of the square. To cut these triangles and have the straight of grain on the long side of the triangle, multiply the square size by 1.414 (see Diagonal Measurements on page 60 for a detailed explanation). For example if the square size is 2½", multiply 2.5" x 1.414 = 3.535 or 3½"). Add 1¼" to 3½" = 4¾". Cut a square that size and cut into quarters diagonally to yield four edge triangles that include ¼" seam allowance on all sides. The Decimal Equivalent Chart on page 62 will help to translate calculator tenths to ruler-friendly numbers. You also have the option of drawing the exact shape on 10-to-the-inch graph paper, adding seam allowance, and making a template.

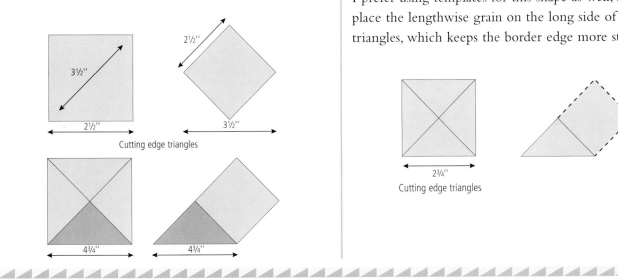

Cutting edge triangles

When adding a Chain of Squares border to a quilt that does not have an automatic fit, I choose a ruler-friendly number for the repeat unit that divides equally into the size of the quilt. If the quilt is 45" square I might choose a repeat unit finished size of 1½" (45" ÷ 1.5" = 30 repeat units per side). This does not mean you can use a 1½" square and turn it on point, because the diagonal measurement of a 1½" square is 2.121 or 2⅛". If I want a 1½" repeat unit size from point to point, I draw a 1½" square on graph paper, mark the center of all four sides and connect the marks to create the square I need. To know the actual size of the square, divide the repeat unit length by 1.414 (1.5 ÷ 1.414 = 1.06 or 1¹⁄₁₆"). In other words, the short sides of this square measure 1¹⁄₁₆" but the distance from point to point is 1½". The actual size of the square will always be smaller than the repeat unit length.

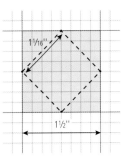

To cut these squares (1¹⁄₁₆" + ½" seam allowance = 1⁹⁄₁₆") my preference would be to draw the square on graph paper, add seam allowance and make a template. If you want to rotary cut the squares, refer to the Decimal Equivalent Chart on page 62 using your calculations.

The edge triangles are created by adding 1¼" to the finished diagonal measurement of the square (1½" + 1¼" = 2¾"). Cut a square 2¾" and cut into quarters diagonally. I prefer using templates for this shape as well, so I can place the lengthwise grain on the long side of all the triangles, which keeps the border edge more stable.

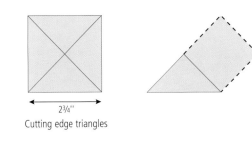

Cutting edge triangles

Each of the four borders ends with smaller triangles. Add whole edge triangles and trim away the excess ¼" from the point of the square. This keeps the straight grain on the appropriate edges.

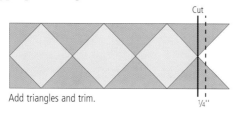

Add triangles and trim.

When constructing this border, press seams away from the squares.

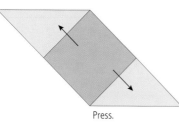

Press.

Corners

The corners most often reiterate the design of the square.

Variations

Any square design can be used in this border. You can also fracture the square space or edge triangles any way you choose.

Samples

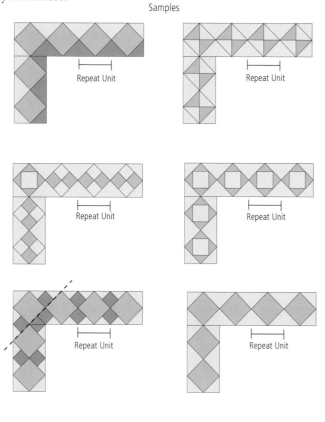

Parallelograms and Twisted Ribbons

Description

Parallelogram and twisted ribbon borders can be directional and/or look similar to a diamond border. The difference between a parallelogram and a diamond is that a diamond has four equal sides and a parallelogram has two equal short sides and two equal longer sides. A parallelogram border is developed by placing two right triangles together or separating the triangles with one or more squares of the same size as the short side of the triangle. This style of border is positioned vertically and companions well with sawtooth borders. For clarity, I have identified a single parallelogram as Repeat Unit 1 and a pair (mirror image) of parallelograms as Repeat Unit 2.

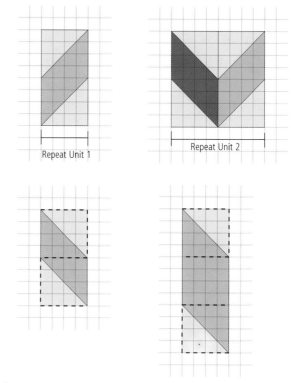

Color

If you are using Repeat Unit 2, it is most effective to use two colors or two values of one color that create high contrast to show depth, definition, and create the illusion that the border undulates.

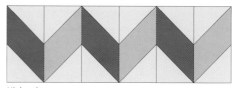

High-value contrast

The triangles on opposite ends of the parallelogram can be the same color and fabric, or each different. If the value and/or color of the edge triangles is similar to what it touches, the parallelograms will appear to float.

Cutting, Piecing, Pressing

To cut and piece both Repeat Units 1 and 2 you will cut a rectangle for the parallelogram and two squares for the edge triangles. The diagonal direction of both seams in the unit is the same. If the finished size of the repeat unit is 1½" x 3", add ½" to both measurements and cut a 3½" x 2" rectangle from the parallelogram fabric and two 2" squares for each edge triangle. Draw a diagonal line on the wrong side of both squares. Piece and press as illustrated. Press seams open when joining units.

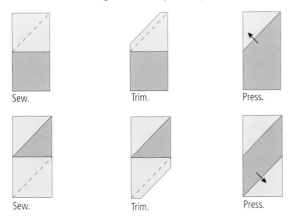

Sew.   Trim.   Press.

Sew.   Trim.   Press.

Repeat Unit 2 is Repeat Unit 1 plus its mirror image. If you are using highly-contrasted fabrics for this unit, half will be one value (the seams will be in one direction) and the other half of the unit will be the remaining fabric or value (its seams will be in the opposite direction). If you are using one fabric, half of the unit will have the seams in one direction and the mirror image will have the seams in the opposite direction. Be consistent, you cannot interchange these two sub-units that make Repeat Unit 2.

When constructing Repeat Unit 2, press both seams in one direction for both units. This will allow easy matching at the intersection when sewing the two mirror images together. Press that seam open. If when sewing the two together you find the seams going in the same direction, just rotate one of them.

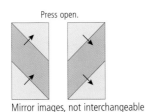

Press open.

Mirror images, not interchangeable

Corners

Repeat Unit 1 is directional. Therefore, to create four corners all the same, you must have an even number of units per side to change direction at the center of all four sides. If you have an odd number of units and want four consistent corners, you can either change direction randomly on each side or add Spacer Borders, page 24, to change the number of repeats from odd to even. Repeat Unit 2 is not directional and can be used pointing upward or downward. In either case, the four corners are the same. The corner piecing does require Y-seam construction to keep the corner square whole.

To draft the corner unit to make the templates, first draw a square the size of the width of the border. Mark the center of all four sides. If your square is not a size easily divisible by two, mark the center of the square by lightly drawing a line diagonally from corner to corner in both directions. Connect the marks as illustrated to develop Shapes 1 (and 1r), 2, and 3. Make templates for Shapes 1, 2, and 3 (turn Shape 1 over for the reverse shape), adding ¼" seam allowance on all sides of each shape.

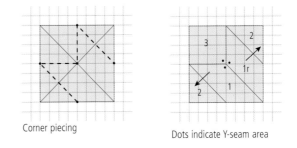

Corner piecing   Dots indicate Y-seam area

1. Cut four each from Shape 1, 1r, and 3. Cut eight from Shape 2.
2. Sew and press Shapes 1 and 1r to Shape 2 as shown.
3. Add to Shape 3; sew from edge to dot and backstitch.
4. Sew Shape 1 and Shape 1r edges together from corner edge to dot and backstitch. Press as shown. Make three more corners.

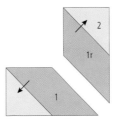

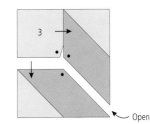

Corner construction   Open

Variations

Hearts on page 11 was a perfect candidate to do a pieced-ribbon border designed from parallelograms. I wanted it to reflect the two colors and values that were in the floating interlocking hearts in the central design, and I wanted the ribbons to float rather than be sewn directly to the edge of the quilt. I also knew this directional border needed an even number of repeat units to create symmetry and four consistent corners. I changed direction in the center and graphed in "ribbon ends." Next, I divided the parallelograms and squares on point into two pieces to reflect the two colors and values.

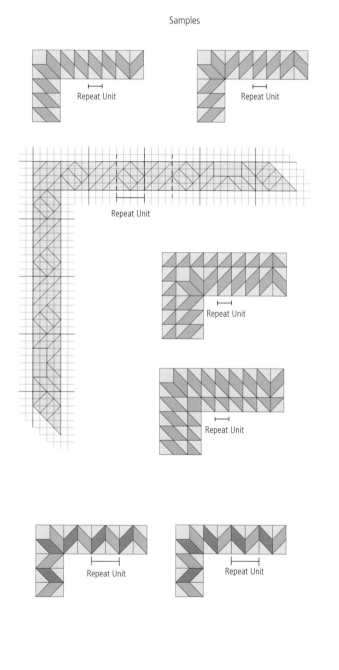

Samples

Repeat Unit

Repeat Unit

Repeat Unit

Repeat Unit

Repeat Unit

Repeat Unit

Repeat Unit

Diamonds
Description

True diamonds have four equal sides. Although quilters often work with 45° and 60° diamonds in patchwork, these two diamond shapes are not drafted on a grid and therefore are not always ruler friendly for figuring out repeat unit sizes. I work with diamonds in a much more simplistic way. *Christmas Rose* on page 26 is made up of 45° diamonds. To create the diamond border, measure the height and width of one diamond in the block (approximately 3⅛" x 1¼"). On graph paper, draw a true rectangle (half as high as it is long) close to that size, in this case 3" x 1½". This is the finished size of the repeat unit. Next mark the center of all four sides of the rectangle and connect the marks. There is the diamond shape with four equal sides. It is not a 45° or a 60° diamond but it feels like the diamond shapes in the blocks because it is a true diamond of approximately the same shape and size and the eye does not notice the slight discrepancy. If you draw a series of repeat units and erase the vertical lines in between, the edge triangles emerge.

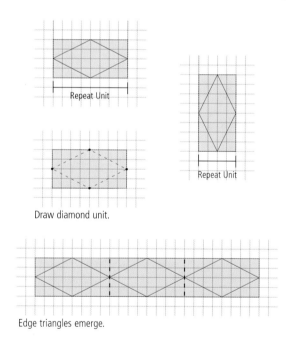

Repeat Unit

Repeat Unit

Draw diamond unit.

Edge triangles emerge.

To make a diamond border that is positioned vertically, do exactly as described above to draft the diamond shape. However, when the diamond is positioned vertically, the repeat unit length is the short edge and a different edge triangle shape emerges when you draw a series of them. If your quilt size is not equally divisible by the size of your repeat unit, add spacer borders, page 24, to bring it up to size.

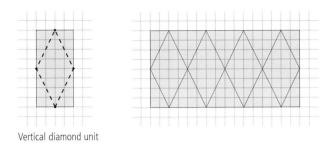

Vertical diamond unit

Color

The colors used for a diamond border can be scrappy and representative of the colors in the central design or a gradated value scheme of one or more colors. The edge triangles can match the value of what they touch to camouflage the seam or can be bold and make a more dramatic statement. Opposite edge triangles can be different colors as well. Experiment.

Cutting, Piecing and Pressing

After you have developed the diamond and edge triangle shapes, make templates. The straight grain should be placed on the outer edge of the border edge triangles. Straight grain placement for the diamond shape is dictated by fabric design first. If this is not a factor, place the straight grain on two parallel edges.

Grain lines

Piece two triangles to each diamond, pressing away from the diamond. When joining these units, open the seam. To create the end triangles, add two edge triangles and trim off excess ¼" beyond the diamond point, which results in the straight grain being placed appropriately.

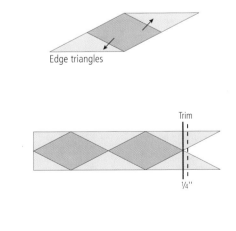

Edge triangles

Trim

¼"

Corners

The corner for the horizontally-positioned diamond is designed by drawing a square the width of the repeat unit. Mark the center of all four sides and connect the marks to create a square on point that gracefully connects the two side borders. Make templates or rotary cut.

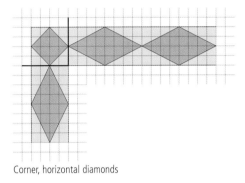

Corner, horizontal diamonds

The corner for the vertically-positioned diamond is designed by drawing a square the width of the repeat unit. Mark the center of all four sides and connect the marks, first vertically then horizontally, to create a four-patch. The A square is left plain, the B square is divided in half diagonally to create a half-square triangle, each of the two C squares are fractured to create three triangles. Press away from the large triangle, keeping the straight grain on the outside edge of all triangles. Make templates for all shapes and assemble as illustrated.

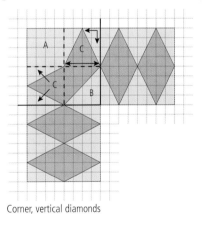

Corner, vertical diamonds

Variations

Design variations are created by fracturing the basic shapes. You can split the diamond shape by placing the template on a strip unit or breaking the diamond shape into four smaller diamonds as I have done in *Star Fire* on page 74. The edge triangles could also be fractured to create more design. Once you have a design, make templates for all shapes. As you continue to fracture space, added opportunities for color, design, and fabric occur.

Samples

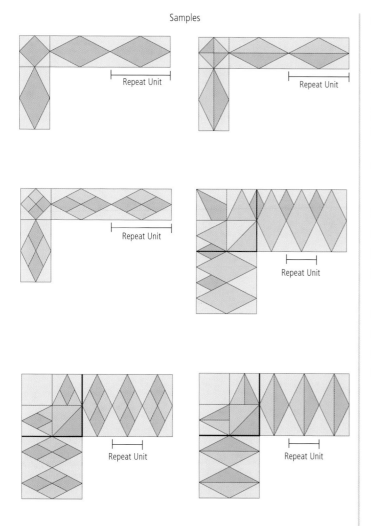

Repeat Unit

Repeat Unit

Repeat Unit

Repeat Unit

Repeat Unit

Repeat Unit

Dogtooth

Description

This non-directional style of border is made from one shape; a triangle that has two sides the same length and the third side longer or shorter. The straight grain is placed on the third side. The triangle I use most often, a right triangle, is twice as long as it is high.

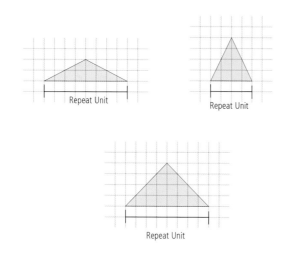

Repeat Unit

Repeat Unit

Repeat Unit

Color

The background and/or color can be on either edge. I often use this border with just two colors, as in *Medallion Sampler* on page 71 and *Diamond Jubilee* on page 64 but you could also make it scrappy or gradate the colors to create movement and shimmer.

Cutting, Piecing, Pressing

To rotary cut the right-angle dogtooth, add 1¼" to the finished size of the long side of the triangle, cut a square that size, and then cut it into quarters diagonally. I prefer to make a template so I can maintain lengthwise grain on the long side of all triangles.

To cut the tall dogtooth, make a template so the reference dots on the fabric can help align the two triangles accurately and keep the lengthwise grain on the short side of the triangles. Press the seams in one direction when you attach the border to the quilt.

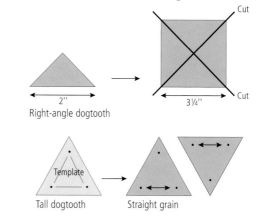

Cut

2"
Right-angle dogtooth

3¼"
Cut

Template
Tall dogtooth

Straight grain

Corners

The corner for the right-angle dogtooth border can be turned by placing a plain square at the corner (although it is added as a triangle; refer to illustration for clarification) or by using a half-square triangle unit at the corner. Notice the difference between the two and whether the triangle that ends at the corner is on the outside edge or the inside edge.

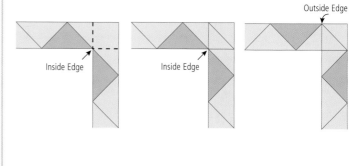

Inside Edge

Inside Edge

Outside Edge

The taller dogtooth border corner can be a plain square or a half-square triangle.

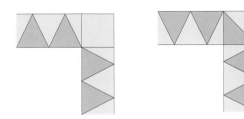

Variations

All the triangles in either of these two styles can also be fractured into more pieces, or consider using a template for the triangle shape and custom cut a design from a border print.

Samples

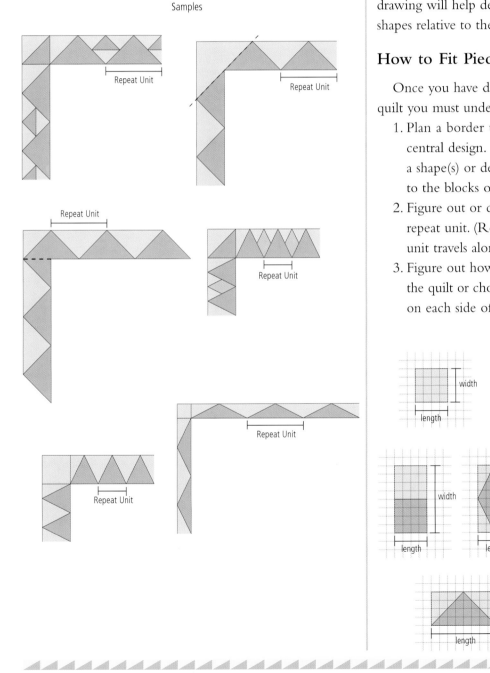

Repeat Unit

Repeat Unit

Repeat Unit

Repeat Unit

Repeat Unit

Repeat Unit

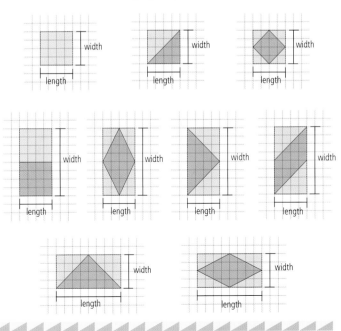

Noteworthy

Whenever you design, draft, or calculate, always work with finished measurements (seam allowances not included). A seam allowance of ¼'' on all sides of each shape is added only when you begin to cut and sew.

Pieced Border Construction

Sketch a complete or partial scale drawing to see the central design. Try different border options and choose the one that best enhances your quilt. Consider the chosen border from both edges. Refer to Design Process beginning on page 66 for additional ideas. A scale drawing will help determine size and proportion of shapes relative to the central design.

How to Fit Pieced Borders to Your Quilt

Once you have decided to add a pieced border to your quilt you must understand and execute the following:

1. Plan a border that enhances and improves your central design. It will be made from repeat units of a shape(s) or design element present in or related to the blocks or central design of the quilt.
2. Figure out or choose the size (finished length) of the repeat unit. (Repeat-unit length is the distance the unit travels along the edge of the quilt.)
3. Figure out how many repeat units fit on each side of the quilt or choose how many repeat units you want on each side of the quilt.

Sampling of Repeat Units

Once you have chosen a repeat unit design, you need to know the finished length of the repeat unit and how many repeat units fit on each side of the quilt.

Notice in #2 on page 57, you either figure out or choose the size of the repeat unit and in #3 you either figure out or choose how many repeat units will be on each side of the quilt.

Whichever one you choose, you must figure out the other. You only need to figure out one part; either the size of the repeat unit or how many repeat units fit on the side of the quilt.

CHOOSING THE SIZE OF REPEAT UNITS

If you choose the repeat-unit size, your task is to figure out how many repeat units fit evenly on the side of the quilt. To do that, let's assume you choose a 1½" sawtooth repeat unit.

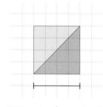

1½" sawtooth repeat unit

To figure out how many repeat units fit per side (60" quilt), divide the finished measurement of the side of the quilt by the finished length of the repeat unit; 60" ÷ 1.5" = 40 repeat units per side. If the quilt is a rectangle measuring 60" x 72", 60" ÷ 1.5" = 40 repeat units for the top and bottom and 72" ÷ 1.5 = 48 repeat units for the two sides of the quilt. This way the size of the repeat unit is easier for me to estimate and determine proportionately, based on the shapes within the central design.

If the size of your repeat unit does not divide into the finished size of your quilt evenly, resulting in a whole number of repeats per side, you have two options.

1. Change the finished size of the repeat unit to one that does divide evenly into your finished quilt measurement.

2. Add spacer borders, referring to page 24.

I usually choose a repeat-unit size smaller (often half) than what appears in the central design. Using a smaller size in the border changes the rhythm of the quilt and lets the viewer know it is a border.

CHOOSING THE NUMBER OF REPEATS

If you choose the number of repeat units you want to fit along the side of the quilt, then your task is to figure out the size of the repeat unit. To do that, let's assume again your quilt is 60" square and you estimate 15 repeat units per side might look good. To figure out what size each of those 15 repeat units will be, divide the quilt size by the number of repeats per side, 60" ÷ 15 units = 4" repeat units. If your quilt is a rectangle measuring 60" x 72", 60" ÷ 15 units = 4" units for the top and bottom borders and 72" ÷ 4" units = 18 repeat units for each of the two side borders. If you divide 72" by 15 units as you did for the top and bottom, the repeat unit size becomes 4.8", not a ruler-friendly number and also larger than the 4" repeat unit size established for the top and bottom. It will be much more appealing to keep the repeat-unit size the same and change the number of repeats for the sides on a rectangle quilt.

If you divide the chosen number of repeats into the finished size of the quilt and the result is a repeat-unit size that is not ruler friendly, change the number of repeats until you get a ruler-friendly number. For example, on a 60" square if you choose 14 repeats per side, 60" ÷ 14 = 4.285", not a ruler-friendly number for the repeat unit. If you change the number of repeats to 15 (60" ÷ 15 = 4") the result is a ruler-friendly number.

Detail of **Floral Fantasy**

Corners

The corners are a square the same dimension as the width of the border. They can be a continuation of the exact side-border piecing or a plain fabric square or you can design a corner. Corners should relate to the side borders in color and/or shape. Graphing them out helps to ensure successful corners.

Ideally, all four corners should be the same. To create four identical corners there are some things to consider, such as whether the pieced border is directional or non-directional and whether an even or odd number of repeat units is necessary to achieve the desired results. If the repeat unit is non-directional the corners will often be identical automatically. So, whether you have an even or odd number of whole repeat units per side is not relative to creating identical corners. An exception might be the checkerboard border if the coloring is more complex than two colors.

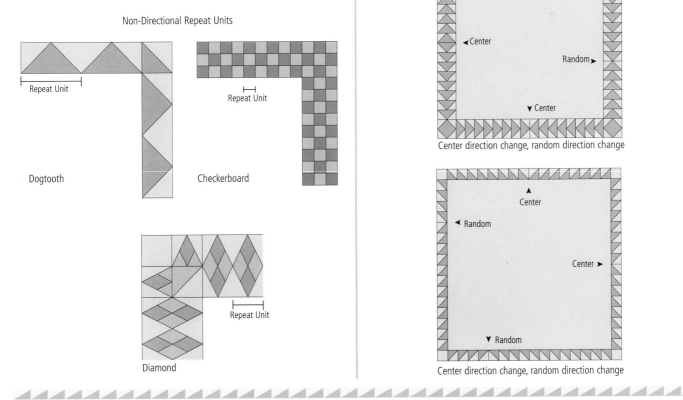

Non-Directional Repeat Units

Dogtooth

Checkerboard

Diamond

If the repeat unit is directional, it can matter whether there are an even or odd number of repeat units.

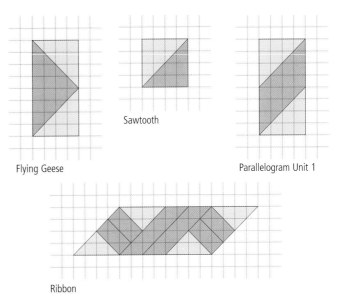

Directional Repeat Units

Flying Geese

Sawtooth

Parallelogram Unit 1

Ribbon

1. If the repeat unit is directional, an even number of units is needed to change direction at the center to create four identical corners. If the number of repeat units is odd, changing direction can be done randomly. The shaded sawtooth border on *Floral Fantasy* on page 73 changes direction randomly.

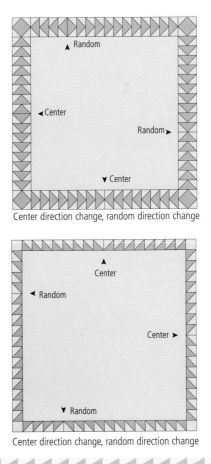

Center direction change, random direction change

Center direction change, random direction change

2. If there are an odd number of directional units you can redesign the center unit to create a direction change or redesign the three center units.

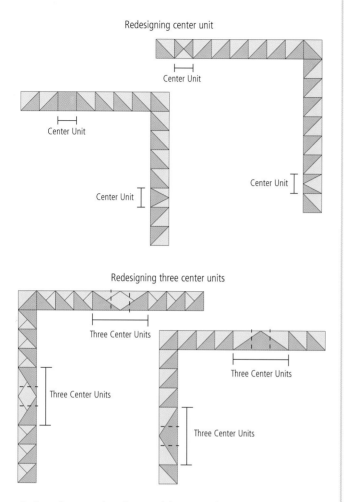

Redesigning center unit

Center Unit

Center Unit

Center Unit

Center Unit

Redesigning three center units

Three Center Units

Three Center Units

Three Center Units

Three Center Units

3. Another option is to add spacer borders one half the finished repeat-unit length, which adds the space of one more unit and brings the number of repeat units from odd to even. This is discussed in more detail in Spacer Borders on page 24.

Corner design options are given with each border style.

Diagonal Measurements

To figure out the diagonal measurement of a square or to figure out the distance of the long side of a half-square triangle, it is important to understand the relationship between the side of a square and its diagonal. The diagonal measurement of a square or half-square triangle is always 1.414 times the side of the square. This "value" is derived from the Pythagorean Theorem, $a^2 + b^2 = c^2$.

Whether you remember that or not isn't as important as understanding the relationship between the side of a square or half-square triangle and its diagonal. This information will enable you to:

- Figure out the size of your quilt if you are setting the blocks on point.
- Figure out what size to cut the setting side triangles and corner triangles and keep the straight of grain on the correct edge(s).
- Know what size the quilt will be when a central design or block is turned on point.
- Figure out the size of the corner triangles that will be added to it.
- Figure out the size of pieced borders that use a square on point.

Noteworthy

You will either be multiplying by 1.414 or dividing by 1.414

1. If you are setting blocks on point and want to figure out what size your quilt will be, first multiply the finished size of one block by 1.414 to find its diagonal distance, then multiply that by the number of blocks across and down in your quilt. If your quilt is three 12" blocks across by four blocks down, set on point, 12" x 1.414 = 16.968" = 17"; 17" x 3 blocks across = 51" wide; 17" x 4 blocks down = 68" long; quilt measures 51" x 68" finished.

2. This same quilt of 12" blocks set on point needs side and corner triangles to complete the design. The side triangles must have straight grain on their long side, which becomes the outside edge of the quilt top. This side triangle, in size and shape, is the diagonal half of one 12" block. Because these side triangles must have the straight grain on their long side, you need to cut quarter-square triangles. To know the size of the square to cut, you add 1¼" to the finished diagonal measurement of one block. For example, the finished diagonal measurement of the 12" block is 17" (12" x 1.414 = 16.968 = 17") + 1¼" = 18¼". Cut a square 18¼" and cut into quarters diagonally to yield four side triangles.

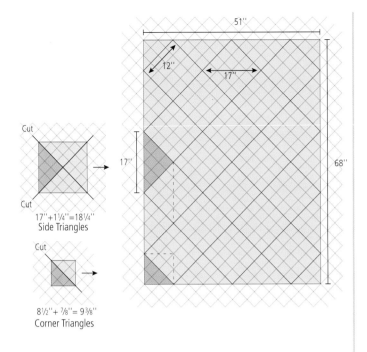

Cut

Cut

17"+1¼"=18¼"
Side Triangles

Cut

8½"+ ⅞" = 9⅜"
Corner Triangles

The four corner triangles needed for the quilt, in size and shape, are one diagonal quarter of one 12" block. The corner triangles must have straight grain on their two short sides, which means you need to cut half-square triangles. To know the size of the square to cut in half diagonally, you divide the size of the block by 1.414 and add ⅞" to that. Cut a square that size and then cut in half diagonally to yield two corner triangles. For example, $12" \div 1.414 = 8.486" = 8\frac{1}{2}" + \frac{7}{8}" = 9\frac{3}{8}"$. Cut a 9⅜" square in half diagonally.

Detail of **Garden Gate**

3. If you have a central-design block that you want to position on point and add triangles onto it to square it again, what size will the quilt be? Multiply the size of the central design block by 1.414, which gives you the diagonal measurement of the central design block and the size of the quilt when you add on the four corner triangles to square it. For example, the central design block measures 24" finished; 24" x 1.414 = 33.936 = 34". That is the diagonal measurement of the center block and the finished size of the quilt when corner triangles are added to it.

4. The corner triangles require straight grain on their two short sides. To know the size of the square to cut in half diagonally, you divide the size of the finished central design block by 1.414 and then add ⅞". For example, 24" ÷ 1.414 = 16.973" = 17" + ⅞" = 17⅞". Cut a 17⅞" square and cut in half diagonally to yield two of the four corner triangles.

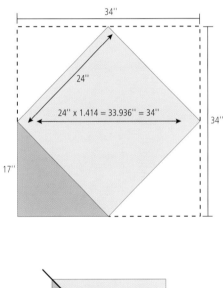

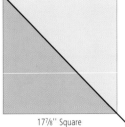

17⅞" Square

5. When planning a pieced border incorporating squares positioned on point, the important measurement or the repeat-unit length is not the short side of the square on point but the distance from point to point diagonally. Decide the distance you want the repeat unit to travel, then draw a square that size, mark the center of all four sides of the square, and connect the marks, which creates a square that travels the desired distance. To know the size of the square to cut, divide the diagonal distance by 1.414, add ¼" seam allowance, and cut the squares. For example a 1" (repeat length unit) ÷ 1.414 = .707" = ⁷⁄₁₀". Draw a ⁷⁄₁₀" square on 10-to-the-inch graph paper, add ¼" seam allowance to it, make a template, and cut the squares.

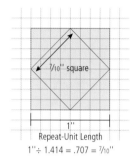

⁷⁄₁₀" square

1"
Repeat-Unit Length
1" ÷ 1.414 = .707 = ⁷⁄₁₀"

Decimal Equivalents

Use this chart to convert calculator numbers to fractions. If you keep 6-, 8-, or 10-to-the-inch graph paper on hand, you can convert fractions to ruler-friendly numbers or draw the shape on appropriate graph paper and make templates. When calculator numbers fall between two numbers, use the fraction it is closest to, or round off to the nearest tenth and go to 10-to-the-inch graph paper and make a template.

Decimal Equivalent Chart

Decimal	Fraction	Decimal	Fraction
.0625	¹⁄₁₆	.5625	⁹⁄₁₆
.1	¹⁄₁₀	.6	³⁄₅
.125	⅛	.625	⅝
.1666	⅙	.6666	⅔
.1875	³⁄₁₆	.6875	¹¹⁄₁₆
.2	⅕	.7	⁷⁄₁₀
.25	¼	.75	¾
.3	³⁄₁₀	.8	⅘
.3125	⁵⁄₁₆	.8125	¹³⁄₁₆
.3333	⅓	.833	⅚
.375	⅜	.875	⅞
.4	⅖	.9	⁹⁄₁₀
.4375	⁷⁄₁₆	.9375	¹⁵⁄₁₆
.5	½		

Measuring Your Patchwork

Measuring your work and maintaining the finished, repeat-unit length is of the utmost importance. To be able to measure your work as you sew, you must understand that pieced borders are created from repeat units: sawtooth units, flying geese units, chain of squares units . . .

The finished repeat-unit length is the distance the unit travels along the edge of the quilt, not necessarily how high it is. The finished, repeat-unit length is what you need to know to measure your work. Finished, repeat-unit length means there is no seam allowance included.

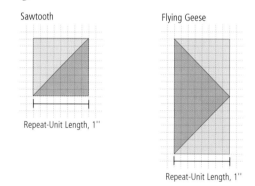

Sawtooth

Repeat-Unit Length, 1"

Flying Geese

Repeat-Unit Length, 1"

Measure your work as you sew. This technique takes a little longer but the rewards are high and it will save you from feeling frustrated and defeated. If you do not measure as you sew, you end up randomly taking in or letting out seams to make the border fit. This resolution is not acceptable because it creates inequality among the shapes and often, bowing of the edge. Take the time to achieve quality work.

Example: 1" finished, repeat-unit length sawtooth border.

1. Sew two 1" sawtooth units together, finger-press, and measure, 2 (units) x 1" (finished-repeat-unit length) = 2" + ½" (seam allowance) = 2½" (correct measurement). If it measures correctly, forget that number. If it does not, correct it, while also examining whether the unit is sewn straight. Continue to sew pairs.

2. Add another pair of sawtooth units to the first pair, finger-press, and measure, 4 (units) x 1" = 4" + ½" (seam allowance) = 4½" (correct measurement). If it measures correctly, forget that number. If it does not, correct it.

If you remain faithful to this concept, you will always know where the problem or discrepancy is because, it must be in the last seam you have sewn. Continue adding units and measuring in this manner.

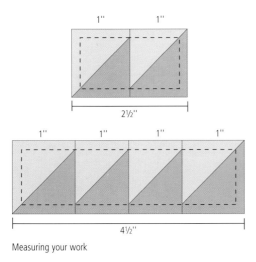

Measuring your work

Automatic-Fit Borders

There are times when borders fit automatically, as in the case of repeat-block quilts. These borders fit automatically when the same shape, size and orientation of the block (on square or on point) elements are used in the border. The finished repeat-unit size you need for the border will be the same as the grid dimension of your blocks. Add ¼" to all sides of each shape for cutting. The size of the border repeat unit can also be half, one quarter, or the same size as the grid dimension.

For example, if I have a repeat block quilt of 6" Churn Dash blocks (3 x 3 grid, 2" finished grid dimension) set on point, I can automatically place the exact same number of squares or repeat units that occur within the block on point for each block in the border. The same is true if the blocks are placed on square. In the case of the Churn Dash, there are three 2" square spaces on point or on square that fit within the block from point to point or along the edge of the block. This means that for every block on point (or on square) positioned in the quilt, three 2" squares fit in the border, or six 1" squares, or twelve ½" squares.

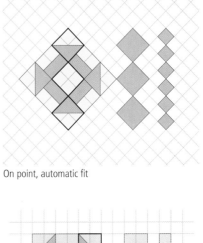

On point, automatic fit

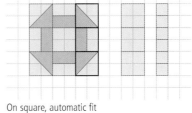

On square, automatic fit

You can take the 2" square on point (or on square) and fracture the space the same as in the block or any way you choose. It could be plain as in Chain of Squares, a half-square triangle as in a Sawtooth border, a four-patch, a quarter-square triangle unit and so on. Once you know the finished size of the repeat unit, you can create your own design within that space. Automatic-fit borders offer the opportunity for color and design without a lot of complicated computations. You could also halve the size of the blocks. You can continue to add pieced or plain borders in this way as long as the widths are related to the grid dimension of the block. This technique can also be used to design pieced sashing between the blocks.

Detail of **Diamond Jubilee**, without completer borders

In *Diamond Jubilee* the primary design is the nine larger stars and the secondary design is the four-patches and small stars. The completer border extends and completes the small stars and four-patches on the edge of the primary design.

In *Kaleidoscope* (page 75) there is no secondary design. The blocks are the primary design and the completer border completes the block design at the edge.

In all three of these examples, the completer border is critical to the completeness of the whole design. Examine your quilt carefully and determine whether or not a completer border is appropriate. They take additional time but are well worth it.

After adding the completer border, additional borders can be added when and if they continue to improve the quilt's design.

Completer Borders

Completer borders are borders added to the quilt to finish or complete the design rather than stopping it abruptly at the quilt edge, making the design appear unfinished or incomplete. Often it is the secondary design of the quilt that needs completion. A scale drawing or sketch helps you see and then identify and design the completer borders. They are not a new design but part of what already exists to extend and complete the design.

Look at the finished quilts referred to here. Then, use an envelope or piece of paper to cover up the completer border to see how each quilt looked before the completer border was added.

In *My Journey* (page 71), the sampler blocks are the primary design and the secondary design is created from the corner detail on each of the sampler blocks, which creates the square on point at the intersections. The completer border completes the square-on point-design.

Diamond Jubilee, 1996, designed, machine pieced and hand quilted by author. A sampling of eight-pointed stars and the added secondary design required a completer border. The addition of the chain of squares, dogtooth, and quilted border put the icing on the cake.

Crossroad, 2003, designed and machine pieced by author, machine quilted by Kathleen Pappas of Los Angeles, CA.
This quilt is a sampling of various borders, several of which echo shapes from the interior design: spacer, corner triangles, sawtooth, border print, checkerboard, narrow, dogtooth, and a final plain fabric mitered border.

DESIGN PROCESS

To explain my approach to designing and adding borders, I will walk you through my thought and action process of designing the borders for *Crossroad*.

My hope in describing my process is to show you how one step follows another, how each border builds individually yet is impacted and influenced by the existing shapes, while staying focused on enhancing the central design and improving the visual impact of the quilt overall. Using the techniques of sketching, scale drawings, a design wall, rough-cut mock-ups in actual size, Polaroid photos, and mirrors all aid the planning process, while still allowing serendipity to occur. Once I see my quilt emerge through this process, I begin to cut and sew.

When I design I always separate color and design from workmanship, which enables me to design freely, without being encumbered by thinking about how I will sew it all together. Once I have a clear idea of my design, using a scale drawing and interviewing color/fabric choices by rough cutting actual-size shapes for a mock-up on the design wall, I have created a map for myself. I then begin to cut and sew. This process does not take a day or two but transpires over time.

Crossroad

This quilt is rather straightforward using a 12" center block (four-patch drafting category, 8 x 8 grid, 1½" grid dimension) that was bordered, turned on point, and then corner triangles and additional borders were added. I chose the center Know It All block because it embraced such a vast variety of shapes that could potentially be repeated in the various border areas.

Border One

When the 12" block was complete, I wanted to add a border that repeated the burgundy triangles to expand the design outward and blur the boxy block edges, as well as include the light blue, dark blue, and burgundy as narrow borders with a border print fabric. This entire border area is 1⅞" wide (¼", ⅜", ⅛", 1⅛" border print), which is the exact height of the burgundy triangle in the block (1½"), plus the ⅜" diagonal measurement of the ¼" border that outlines the triangle. Notice that I used only a partial

width of the border print based on the space available to me in the border. I used envelopes to section off different 1⅛" areas to interview and evaluate design options to make a final choice. See Border Prints beginning on page 26 for more detailed information.

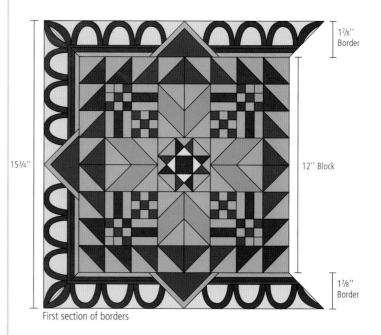

First section of borders

Border Two (Spacer Border)

Setting a block on point and adding corner triangles brings it back to a square and the size of that square is the diagonal measurement (page 60) of the block. I wanted the size of that square to be evenly divisible by 1½", which is the grid dimension of the center block and therefore the proportionate repeat-unit size to begin designing with. The diagonal measurement of the 15¾" quilt top is 22.270 or 22¼" (15.75" x 1.414 = 22.270), which is not evenly divisible by 1½". I needed to increase the size of the existing quilt top to a larger number that when multiplied by 1.414 is a diagonal measurement evenly divisible by 1½". By increasing the block size in small increments I found the diagonal measurement of 17" is 24.038 or 24", which is evenly divisible by 1½" (24" ÷ 1½" = 16 repeat units). The difference between 15¾" and 17" is 1¼". Half of that (⅝") is the total finished width of each spacer border (page 24) I needed to add to all four sides of the quilt top. I subdivided that space into a ⅜" burgundy border and a ¼" blue border to bring my quilt top up to a 17" square, which when placed on point and with corners added, became a 24" square.

Border Three (Corner Triangles)

To plan my piecing within that space I needed to know the size of the corner triangles (pages 40-41). I made a scale drawing (page 14) of a 24" square, placed a square on point within that space and it became obvious that the two short sides of the corner triangles are 12" and the long side is 17" because it attaches to the 17" center design. Another way to know the size of the corner triangles is to divide 17" (the size of the bordered central design) by 1.414, which equals 12.022 or 12". I then knew the size of the triangle and could design within that space.

My options for designing within the corner triangle area were obvious because the center block offered abundant opportunities such as sawtooth, checkerboards, flying geese, and a border print. To create a harmonious balance between design and color I took what already existed and rearranged it, rather than adding new design elements.

My initial ideas to fill the corner triangle area were to include a 1½" sawtooth border, repeat the burgundy triangle with the blue outline, and repeat the border print fabric in the same width used previously in Border One. I decided to place the sawtooth border toward the outer edge of the corner triangle, away from the border-print edge because when they were placed next to each other, the result was busy and chaotic. On my scale drawing I began to fill in the corner triangle space, trying ideas in one corner triangle and making changes in another to actually see, proportionately, what I liked.

Once I got a pretty good design on paper I translated that to my design wall by placing the central design on point and rough cutting the sawtooth border in actual size and placing them in position to create a mock-up to see how it would look and to decide color. I decided to change the size of the sawtooth border from 1½" to half of that (¾") because the larger sawteeth drew too much attention.

Border Three

At this time I also determined what color the sawteeth would be by trying both blue and burgundy alone and then a mixture of both. It became apparent to me that keeping them blue and consistent with the central design created both repetition and unity.

This illustrates the value of scale drawings and design-wall mock-ups before you cut and sew! My drawing also helped me determine the proportionate size of the burgundy triangles. Initially I drew it much too small. I continued to fill in the remaining space with plain fabric and the border print.

Once I'm using the design wall, I begin to take Polaroid photos. I mock up one corner, photograph that area and then place mirrors on the photos appropriately to see the whole quilt. I only need to design one corner I like and then I continue to design and add borders.

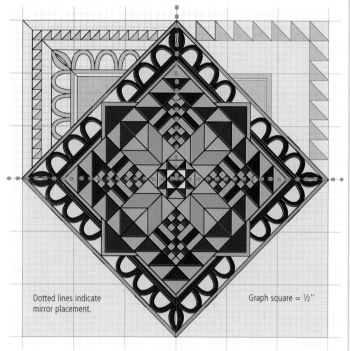

Dotted lines indicate mirror placement.

Graph square = ½"

Designing corners; determining size and proportion using scale drawing and mirrors

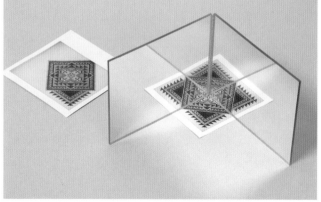

Using Polaroids and mirrors; triangles too big

Border Four (Checkerboard)

The checkerboard border was inspired by the Nine-Patches. Using the same grid size of the Nine-Patches for the border checkerboard was too large. I decided to use half of the ¾" grid (⅜") used for the sawtooth border, which also created an automatic fit (page 63) without number crunching. I kept the color of the checkerboard consistent with the central design Nine-Patch area although the fabrics are different. My quilt measures 25½" after adding the checkerboard border (24" plus an additional 1½" for the four ⅜" grids for the checkerboard).

Checkerboard added

Border Five (Dogtooth)

I wanted to incorporate a flying geese border to repeat that shape from the central design. After drawing and experimenting, I decided that because the triangle in the block was not positioned as a flying geese unit, it looked out of place positioned that way in the border. Therefore I positioned it with the long side of the triangle as its base as a dogtooth border. I liked how this looked and after some mocking up of color, again decided to go with blue rather than burgundy because it was now well established that burgundy was secondary in importance to blue. This decision was also influenced by my preference for a blue final border rather than burgundy.

Now that I knew the orientation and color of the repeat unit I would use, I needed to know the size. The diagonal measurement of 1½" (the grid dimension of the center block) is 2.121. Referring to the Decimal Equivalent Chart on page 62, .121 is very close to .125, which translates to ⅛". When I divided 25.5" (the size of my quilt after the checkerboard border is added) by 2.125" (2⅛") my answer was 12. Twelve triangles having the straight grain on the long edge of the triangle fit exactly on each edge of the quilt. To cut these triangles I added 1¼" to 2⅛" (3⅜") and cut squares, then cut them into quarters diagonally to yield four triangles per square. The corner squares are the same size as the width of the borders and the width of the border is half the size of the long side of the triangles (half of 2⅛" is 1 1/16"). Once this border was added onto the quilt, the quilt measured 27⅝" (25½" + 1 1/16" + 1 1/16" = 27⅝").

Dotted lines indicate mirror placement.

Border Six (Final Borders)

I then added a narrow border of burgundy and the border print again to maintain continuity. Instead of using only half the width of the border print I eventually decided to use the entire width of the design. Following the border print I added burgundy, then light blue, then a final blue border to conclude the design. When it came time to bind the quilt, I added a narrow border of the blue before the burgundy binding which makes the quilt visually more complete.

Paws and Reflect, 2003, designed and machine pieced by author. Machine quilted by Jill Schumacher, Weed, CA. What started out as a simple Bear Paw quilt evolved into a more complex design with the addition of an interlocking square design, half stars reflecting the center star, and a pieced border of small individual paws. A border print was incorporated to outline shapes and areas, as well as using it as an appliqué border to add a curved element that then inspired the scalloped edge that follows the curved shape of the quilting design.

Medallion Sampler, 1997, designed, machine pieced, and hand quilted by author. In a typical medallion style, multiple borders enhance the center design area beginning with pieced side triangles, a shaded sawtooth border on each side of a plain-fabric quilted border, narrow and dogtooth borders, and a final plain-fabric mitered border.

Pinwheels, 1996, designed, machine pieced, and hand quilted by author. The two sizes of pinwheels are surrounded by my "homemade" border print consisting of a stripe, repeat motif, and floral fabrics separated by narrow borders.

My Journey, 2001, designed, machine pieced, and hand quilted by author. A completer border, multiple chain of squares (each fracturing the square differently and cutting the side triangle shape from a border print), and a final, plain-fabric quilted border make the quilt complete.

Shadow Baskets, 1996, designed, machine pieced, hand appliquéd, and quilted by author. Pieced blocks and a sawtooth border are combined with swags, rounded corners, and the detail of the piping/binding edge finish.

Rhapsody in Bloom, 2002, designed, pieced, appliquéd, and quilted by Country Crossroads Quilt Guild, Modesto, CA, photograph by William Compton, Modesto CA. This is a wonderful pairing of appliqué and piecing. The flying geese border flies around the edge, finishing it beautifully.

Star Crossed, 1992, designed, machine pieced, and hand quilted by author. Simple sawtooth stars are elevated when combined with an alternate block that gives the quilt a diagonal feel. Completer, spacer, and chain of squares borders are used before a light, plain-fabric border is added to float the design.

Baskets, 1996, designed, machine pieced, and hand quilted by author. This quilt incorporates narrow and pieced borders, pieced corner triangles, border prints, and a curved-edge finish to enhance the simple baskets.

Skating by Snowlight, 1991, designed, machine pieced, hand appliquéd, and hand quilted by Nadine Thompson, Pleasanton, CA. A charming quilt design with an appliquéd, symmetrical, undulating repeat-curve vine with stars that travels around the quilt's edge.

Floral Fantasy, 2002, designed and machine pieced by author. Machine quilted by Margaret Gair, San Ramon, CA. This quilt takes the center, on-point block and surrounds it with a shaded sawtooth border that changes direction randomly to create four corners the same. Pieced corner triangles are added before a final series of narrow and border-print borders.

Star Fire, 2003, designed, machine pieced, and hand quilted by author. An example of a pieced diamond border, border print, narrow border, and a final plain-fabric border that is scalloped following the shape of the quilting design.

Kaleidoscope, 2001, designed, machine pieced and quilted by author. In this quilt the pieced blocks are extended out and completed in the first border. The border also combines two colors in two values for added design, detail, and a bit of whimsy.

Epicenter, 1994, designed, machine pieced, and hand quilted by Judy Mathieson, Sebastopol, CA. Photograph by Jack Mathieson, Sebastopol, CA. Multiple rows of a checkerboard-style border wrap around a beautiful, striking, original design.

Gizmo, 2000, designed, machine pieced, and quilted by author. The simplistic woven-border style adds to the contemporary flavor of this repeat-block design.

Double Wedding Ring, 1997, designed, machine pieced, and hand quilted by author. This romantic, traditional pattern takes on a completely different and updated look when its naturally curved edges are appliquéd onto a straight border.

Twilight, 1997, designed, machine pieced, and hand quilted by author. A typical medallion quilt incorporating numerous styles of borders: chain of squares; sawtooth; narrow, corner triangles; half-repeat blocks; a border print; and a final, plain-fabric border.

Desert Stars, 2002, designed, pieced, and machine quilted by Nancy Rink, Bakersfield, CA. Flying geese and checkerboard borders surround the center Lone Star. Smaller stars follow, ending with a second flying geese border that completes the entire design.

Stepping Out, 1995, designed and machine pieced by author, hand quilted by Sheree Cowley, Simi Valley, CA. This contemporary twist on a traditional design is surrounded by both a double row of two sizes of sawteeth, a border print, and a whole-fabric border.

Star of Bethlehem, 1988, designed, machine pieced, and hand quilted by Laura Nownes, Pleasant Hill, CA. and Diana McClun, Walnut Creek, CA. This beautiful, traditional design is surrounded by multiple Sawtooth Star blocks, which are separated to give a more airy feel to the quilt.

Key Chain, 1996, designed and machine pieced by author. This quilt uses an automatic-fit, repeat-block border in addition to multiple plain-fabric and narrow borders.

PLANNING EDGE FINISHES

Purpose and Function

Edge finishing is the final design element and color opportunity for your quilt. Give it adequate, careful consideration.

The edge finish can be applied to the quilt in the form of a binding, a facing, or a piping (or a combination of those finishes). The edge finish can also be self-created by either bringing the backing to the front; or sewing all layers together, then turning it inside out like an envelope or pillow; or creating a knife-edge finish by folding the quilt top and backing edges inward, then sewing them to each other, which encloses the batting.

Applied finishes can be cut from the straight grain of fabric (crosswise grain or lengthwise grain), which is appropriate for wall and display quilts that have straight edges and squared or angled corners. Applied finishes, cut from the bias grain of fabric, are appropriate for all quilts because of their durability, but necessary for edges that are curved or rounded. I also use bias-cut finishes when the fabric print invites it, like stripes, plaids, or checks, to enhance the design.

Fine finishing is the icing on the cake; so important to the visual taste. Look over the following pages, choose a finish that makes your quilt the best it can be, and bring it to a beautiful conclusion.

Noteworthy

Whatever edge finish you select, think it through carefully and determine how much area you need to leave unquilted (if any) to comfortably manipulate and create the edge finish you have selected.

There are numerous ways to finish the edge of your quilt. When choosing the method and style of the edge finish, consider the quilt's character, its purpose, and your personal skill level. If you are making a quilt that is handled, laundered, and used often, like a baby quilt or bed quilt, you might choose a double-fold bias binding, which will be the most durable. If the quilt is for display only, you might choose one of the many options that are less durable but add to the design, color, and visual pleasure, like a single-fold binding or facing, a piping, or a curved or scalloped edge.

Do not rush this part of the quiltmaking process. It is very important to the overall look and integrity of the whole quilt to take your time. Always ask yourself if the quilt will be visually improved with the edge finish you have selected. If the answer is yes, then take the time to do it well.

If you are making a wall quilt with straight edges for display only, straight-grain binding might be appropriate, even single fold rather than double fold to reduce the bulk. Consider adding details like piping alone or piping combined with binding. If the quilt consists of mostly straight, geometric lines, consider creating a curved or scalloped edge or rounded corners for balance and added softness to the design or by following your quilting design at the outer edge to create the curved or scalloped edge.

If making a very small or miniature quilt, consider applying ⅛"-wide single-fold binding for more appropriate proportion and less bulkiness.

Edge-Finish Selections

Applied Edge Finishes

Applied edge finishes are those that require a separate piece of fabric that is added to the quilt and enclose the edges or a separate piece of fabric placed between the quilt top and backing.

STRAIGHT-GRAIN BINDING

Cut from either the crosswise or lengthwise grain of fabric, it can be individual strips, continuous length, single fold (traditional), or double fold (French). Used on straight edges and corners, it is not suitable for curves and is considerably less durable than bias.

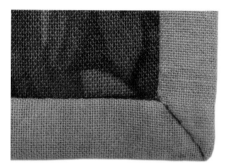

Straight-grain continuous binding; Folded, mitered corner

BIAS BINDING

Cut from the bias grain of the fabric, it can be individual strips, continuous length, single fold (traditional), or double fold (French). Bias grain offers maximum durability and flexibility. It can be used on any quilt but must be used on curves. Stripes and checks cut on the bias add design opportunities.

Checks

Curves

Stripes

Scallops

Rounded corners

INDIVIDUAL STRIP BINDING

Cut from either the straight or bias grain of fabric, four strips are sewn individually to the four sides of the quilt top, then four boxed corners are formed.

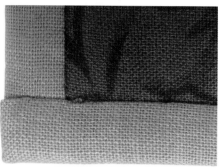

Straight-grain, individual-strip binding; Boxed corner

SINGLE-FOLD BINDING

It covers the quilt edge with a single layer of fabric and subsequently creates less bulk. Single-fold binding is referred to as traditional binding and can be cut from the straight grain or bias grain of fabric and is less durable than double-fold binding.

DOUBLE-FOLD BINDING

Double-fold binding covers the quilt edge with two layers of fabric and is also referred to as French binding. It can be cut from the straight grain or bias grain of fabric and is more durable than single-fold binding.

FACING

Cut from either straight or bias grain of fabric. The facing adds some stability to the edge but is not as durable as binding. It is a good choice for any display quilt edge, especially irregular edges and curves.

Irregular edge, faced; Front

Irregular edge, faced; Back

Straight edge, faced; Front

Back

PIPING

Piping is created by covering thin cording with either a straight- or bias-grain strip of fabric. The cording is tucked into the fold and held in place by stitching right next to it through both layers of fabric. Piping can be applied to the quilt edge alone or in combination with binding.

Piping and piping/binding combination

Self-Created Edge Finishes

A self-created edge finish is one that uses the quilt top and backing, separately or together, to finish the edge.

BACK TO FRONT

This edge requires the backing to be larger than the batting and quilt top. It is created by bringing the backing fabric over the batting to the front of the quilt.

Back to Front; Mitered corner

Back to Front; Boxed corner

ENVELOPE OR PILLOWCASE

An envelope or pillowcase edge is completely finished before the quilting is started. The quilt top, batting, and backing are sewn together, turned right-side out, and hand stitched closed.

Envelope/Pillowcase, squared and rounded corners

KNIFE EDGE

The knife edge is finished by turning under ¼" on both the quilt top and backing edges then hand or machine sewing their edges together.

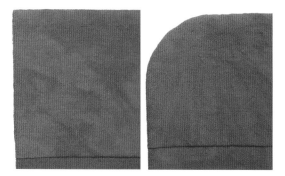

Knife Edge with squared corner and rounded corners

Color and Fabric

The edge finish, if applied, is the final opportunity to add design, color, and visual texture. The goal is to find a color and fabric print that improves your quilt and makes it better than it is without it. Resist rushing this process.

Interview different color and fabric options. One way to interview different choices is to lay your quilt out on a flat surface and fold one edge under at the drawn line (or the eventual finished edge), then lay possible choices under the quilt, exposing only the desired width of the binding. You could also rotary cut ¼" strips of possible choices and lay them on your quilt, then place a piece of white paper up to the strip edge to get a good viewing of how the quilt would look with that fabric and color as its binding. Work near a corner and place a mirror at a 45° angle to see how the binding would look on two edges.

Interviewing binding choices using a mirror

Consider using the final border fabric for the binding to create a smooth, uninterrupted finish. See *Paws and Reflect* on page 70 and *Star Fire* on page 74.

Examine your quilt and consider its colors. Is there one color that is most noticeable that you might want to repeat in the binding? One that is too strong and you do not want to use it? Is the accent color the perfect choice? Explore your options, interview them all, and make an informed choice.

Consider using a stripe, check, or plaid cut on the bias, even if you do not have any curved edges. These prints have the potential to create movement and add charm and unexpected detail to any quilt. One way to see how they look ahead of time is to cut a ¼" or ⅛" tunnel in a 3" x 5" index card and place it on the fabric at a 45° angle to a straight edge.

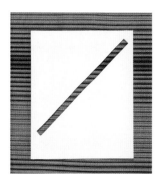

Interviewing fabrics for bias binding

Preparing the Quilt for Edge Finishing

Properly preparing your quilt and its edges for a self-created finish or applied finish is critical to the end result. Before finishing the edge of the quilt, it must have straight sides and square corners. Even if you are curving or scalloping the edge, you must begin with a perfect square or rectangle to develop and mark the curves. Do not trim away the excess batting and backing, but do remove any basting.

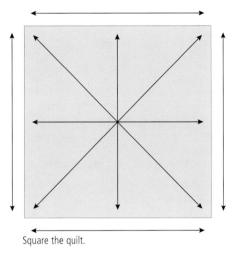

Square the quilt.

If there is a discrepancy, (and more often than not there is) mist the quilt to slightly dampen it. A discrepancy of more than ½" is difficult to correct and can put undue stress on the seams of the quilt, so proceed with caution.

Smooth, pin, and encourage the problem areas straight, creating the same measurement in all areas, both horizontally and vertically, using a tape measure that does not stretch. If the edges are longer than the center measurement I pat and ease them inward to align with the center. If the edges are shorter than the center measurement, I pat, smooth, and carefully stretch the edges outward to align with the center measurement. When doing this, start the adjustment from the inside of the quilt so the discrepancy is distributed over the entire quilt. Keep re-measuring to be sure the quilt is straight and has 90° corners.

Also measure the quilt diagonally from corner to corner. These two measurements should be the same. When the quilt is squared to meet your standards, pin it to the carpet, sheet, or towels. Let it dry completely. A floor fan will speed up the drying process.

Because the final plain border is generously wide, determine how much of the final border you want to see finished and add ¼" (or whatever you decide), to that measurement for the binding seam allowance. Place the horizontal and vertical lines of a square ruler on the last seam connected to the final border on a corner of the quilt. The 45° line of the ruler should be on the miter seam of the border and/or directed through the corner to the center of the quilt. Draw or chalk a line around the corner of the ruler on all four corners of the quilt.

Now take a longer ruler and connect those corner lines, checking to be sure you are always the same distance from the seam. This drawn line must be thin, straight, and accurate, since you will eventually bind to this line.

Once you have drawn this line, your quilt is square. Hand baste around the quilt with small stitches, just outside the drawn line, compressing the three layers together to prevent them from flaring, maintain the straightness of the line you have drawn, and stabilize the edge.

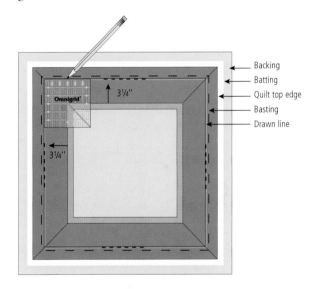

The quilt is now straight, squared, and the edge is ready to finish in whatever style you have chosen. If you are applying binding, facing, or piping, think of the drawn line as the edge of the quilt and align the raw edges of your edge finish to the drawn line. If you are finishing your quilt with one of the three self-created edge finishes, go to that chapter for specific details.

Correcting the Wave

Once the edges of your quilt are finished, lay it out flat or hang it and do any finish blocking and straightening it might need. No matter how careful you are, occasionally you will get a slight wave or wobble on the edge of the quilt after it is completely finished.

Sometimes you can correct very slight discrepancies by careful steaming from the back, by laying the quilt face down on a clean, soft surface and skimming the iron over the border area, not touching the iron to the fabric, just getting close enough that the steam is directed onto the fabric. This often corrects small discrepancies if the batting is cotton or wool.

If that does not work, try slightly dampening the quilt, then moving and manipulating it with your hands to encourage seams and edges to be flat and straight, constantly checking corners for squareness. Pin in place to hold the new shape and let it air dry.

Another tried-and-true technique to create flat edges is to slightly gather in the excess that creates wavy edges without creating any pleats. To do this, ideally the quilt should hang free from a sleeve. If that is not possible, lay the quilt right-side up on a smooth, flat surface (wood floor, table top, etc.) that will not cling to the quilt (like carpet does) and allow it to "pretend" to be flat. Identify the specific areas that need to be corrected or improved, or you could go around the entire quilt, stitching each side separately. I do not go around corners with this technique but rather stop and start away from the corners to maintain their squareness.

1. Thread a needle (I use a regular betweens quilting needle) with quilting thread the exact color of the fabric next to the binding. Knot the thread as usual, bury it in the batting as you would to begin quilting, and have the needle exit out the seam that joins the last border and the binding.

2. Take approximately ¼" stitches positioned tightly and blindly almost in the seam. The needle enters the fabric just next to where it exits and the ¼" length of the stitch is in the batting, not on top of the quilt. The stitches stay in the quilt top and batting; do not go through to the back of the quilt. Take several stitches in and out at a time, pulling the needle out after each stitch but not extending the thread. Then pull the thread through, extending it and giving a very gentle tug as you do. This action ever so gently gathers in the excess. The waves and ripples will disappear.

3. End by knotting off and burying it as if you were quilting.

Choosing Fabric Grain

I recommend using only 100% cotton fabric for applied bindings. The grain in fabric is the lengthwise (warp) and crosswise (weft) threads that are woven together to create the cloth. Crosswise grain runs from selvage to selvage and has some stretch. Lengthwise grain runs parallel to the selvage and has very little, if any, stretch. Both crosswise and lengthwise grains are described as straight grain. True bias grain runs 45° to the cross and lengthwise grain and has the maximum amount of stretch. Applied edge finishes can be cut from either the straight grain or the bias grain of fabric and each has its own properties, character, and advantages pursuant to specific scenarios.

Straight Grain

Straight-grain edge finishes can be used on wall quilts with straight edges and squared corners. They are cut in crosswise or lengthwise strips and then joined together to create a continuous length of binding or facing, or cut and left as individual strips, depending on the edge finish you choose and whether you will create a folded miter on the corner or a boxed corner. Straight-grain binding will have little or no stretch, will not maneuver around curves and is less durable than bias-cut binding because the threads on straight-grain binding run parallel to the quilt's edge, and if a thread breaks on the fold, the whole binding is essentially broken. Whenever you use a self-created edge finish you are automatically creating a straight-grain finish because your quilt top and backing edges are cut on the straight grain. When cutting straight-grain strips for binding, cut all strips either on the crosswise grain or lengthwise grain. Do not mix the two as the color can appear different due to how the light reflects off of them, and their stretch capabilities are different.

Bias Grain

True bias grain is cut at 45° from the warp and weft threads of the fabric and has the maximum amount of stretch. Binding, facing, or piping cut on the bias lays smooth, can easily go around any curve, or can be mitered at the corners. The threads of bias grain cross over each other and intertwine, resulting in a more durable edge finish for your quilt.

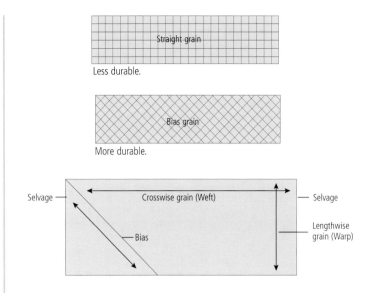

Straight grain
Less durable.

Bias grain
More durable.

Selvage — Crosswise grain (Weft) — Selvage
Bias
Lengthwise grain (Warp)

Establishing the Length and Width of Binding

To know how much binding length you need to go around your quilt, measure the length and width of your quilt, add those two numbers together, double it, then add an additional 12" for corner folds and connecting the ends. If you are binding a curved edge, use a flexible tape measure and measure around the curves from the center of one side to the corner and multiply that by eight plus 12" for a square quilt. On a rectangular quilt, measure from the center of one short side, around the corner to the center of one long side and multiply by four plus 12". For repeat scallops, use a flexible tape measure and measure one scallop and one corner. Multiply each relative measurement by the number of scallops and four corners, add those two numbers together and add 12".

To know how wide to cut your binding you must consider three things:

1. Are you applying single-fold (traditional) or double-fold (French) binding?
2. The seam allowance can determine the finished width you will see on the edge of your quilt. If you want a wider binding to show but will apply it with a ¼" seam allowance, the batting and backing must extend beyond the quilt edge the difference between the ¼" seam allowance and the finished width you desire.
3. The accumulated thickness of the seam allowances and batting, plus the quilt top and backing fabrics.

It is very important for the binding to be filled completely, all the way out to the crease of the binding. If the binding is not full, wear will occur much faster and it will fare poorly if placed in competition. I have made numerous samples using various seam allowances and widths of binding and have found the measurements given in the charts below work beautifully for me using cotton fabrics with either cotton or wool batting and sewing accurately with the suggested seam allowance. The binding will be full once it is wrapped over the edge of the quilt and secured to the back of the quilt with hand stitches, just covering the machine stitching line. This results in a snug fit. To create a binding width other than those shown in the charts, a general rule of thumb to follow to figure out how wide to cut double-fold binding using a ¼" seam allowance is to multiply the finished width of the binding by four and then add ⅞" for seam allowance and fold over. For single-fold binding, multiply the finished width of the binding by two and then add ⅝". I like snug fitting binding so remember this is a generality, it is always wise to make your own sample before cutting all your binding fabric.

Single-Fold (Traditional) Binding

Single-fold binding wraps around the quilt's edge with one thickness of fabric. It can be cut from the straight or bias grain of the fabric.

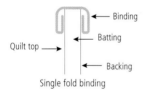

Single fold binding

SEAM ALLOWANCE	FINISHED BINDING WIDTH	CUT WIDTH OF FABRIC STRIP
⅛"	⅛"	¾"
¼"	¼"	1⅛"
½"	½"	1⅞"

Double-Fold (French) Binding

Double-fold binding wraps around the quilt's edge with two thicknesses of fabric. It can be cut from either straight- or bias-grain fabric. Once the binding strips are cut and joined, if making continuous binding, develop a 45° angle on the beginning tail and press in half lengthwise, wrong-sides together.

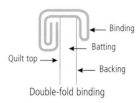

Double-fold binding

SEAM ALLOWANCE	FINISHED BINDING WIDTH	CUT WIDTH OF FABRIC STRIP
¼"	¼"	1⅞"
½"	½"	3"

Fabric Requirements

Once you have determined the width and length of the binding needed, you need to determine how much fabric is required.

Continuous, Straight-Grain Binding from a Rectangle (Regular Yardage)

This style of binding is appropriate for straight edges and corners only. To determine how much fabric is needed to cut enough strips to join together for a continuous length of straight-grain binding, divide the total number of linear inches by the width of the fabric (subtract 3" from the width of your fabric to allow for the waste created when joining the strips diagonally, mitering corners, and joining the ends). For example, if you need a total of 170" of straight grain binding, 170" ÷ 39" (42" wide fabric minus 3" for waste) = 4.36 strips, rounded up to 5 strips needed. Now multiply the number of strips needed by the width of your binding, 5 x 1⅞" (1.875) = 9.375" rounded up to 10" means you need 10" of fabric.

Continuous Bias Binding from a Square

Bias binding looks wonderful on all edges and is necessary to go around any curved edge. Bias binding is more durable than straight-grain binding, lays smoothly, and is just as easy to cut and apply as straight-grain binding. To figure out how large a square of fabric you need that will yield the amount of continuous binding desired, on a calculator, multiply the width of the cut binding by the length. For example 1⅞" (1.875")-wide binding x 200" length needed = 375, which is the total number of square inches needed to make your binding. Now you must find the square root of that number by simply pressing the square root $\sqrt{}$ button on the calculator (the square root of 375 is 19.365, rounded up equals 20"). You need a 20" square to make your 200" of 1⅞"-wide continuous bias binding.

If you want to approximate how much length of continuous bias binding can be cut from a known square size, multiply the length by the width of the square, which gives you the area of the square. Now divide the area of the square by the width of the binding. For example, if you have a 15" square and want to make 1⅞"-wide binding, 15" x 15" = 225" divided by 1⅞" (1.875") = 120" of 1⅞"-wide binding can be cut from a 15" square (approximately).

Individual Bias Strips from a Square

If you want to make continuous bias binding but do not want to make it using either of the tube methods described on pages 88–89 and would rather cut individual strips of bias and join them, you need to be able to estimate how much bias length you can obtain from a square of fabric. To do this, first estimate the total number of straight-grain linear inches that can be obtained from a square by dividing the size of the square by the width of the strips (gives you the number of strips you can cut from the square) then multiply that by the size of the square. The answer is the total number of linear inches of straight-grain binding. The amount of bias will be a little less than that. For example, if you have a 12" square and want 1⅞"-wide bias binding, 12" ÷ 1⅞" (1.875) = 6.4 strips, rounded down to 6 strips x 12" = 72 linear inches of straight-grain binding. The 12" square would yield a little less than 72 linear inches of bias. To cut the square into bias strips that then get joined end to end to create the continuous-bias binding, see pages 88–89.

APPLIED FINISHES

Binding

Continuous, Straight-Grain Binding

Once you have cut enough straight-grain binding strips (all from either crosswise grain or lengthwise grain) to go around your quilt plus an extra 12", join the strips, end to end, to create a continuous length. Join binding strips with a diagonal seam because it is less noticeable than a straight seam, and is less bulky. One exception would be when a fabric print or design is more suitable for a straight-seam connection, like a border print or a stripe. Another exception might be the character of the quilt (Amish style, folk art, primitive).

Place the strip ends at a 90° angle to each other, draw a diagonal line, pin, sew on the line with matching thread and small stitches, press the seams open, and trim.

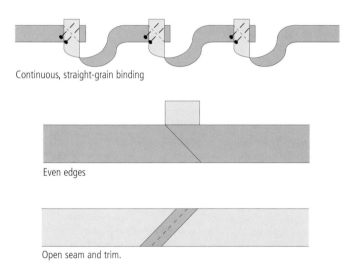

Continuous, straight-grain binding

Even edges

Open seam and trim.

If you are making single-fold binding, draw a line ½" from one long edge, fold the raw edge to meet the line and press. This is the edge that is hand sewn to the back of the quilt once the opposite edge is machine stitched to the edge of the quilt. Cut a 45° angle on the beginning tail.

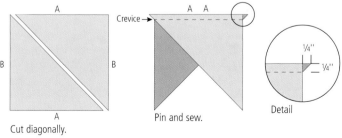

½" — Single-fold binding — Fold and press. — ¼"

If making double-fold binding, cut a 45° angle on the beginning tail and press in half lengthwise, wrong sides together.

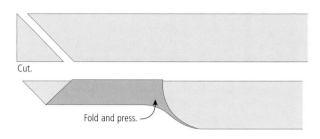

Cut.

Fold and press.

Continuous, Bias-Grain Binding

I offer two similar but slightly different methods for making a bias tube to cut continuous bias binding. Both methods work beautifully and will show you exactly where and how to match the edges for sewing. I have also included how to cut individual bias strips that can be joined end to end to create continuous bias binding.

Noteworthy

When making a bias tube, always sew straight-grain edges together and cut bias-grain edges. You must position your fabric to look exactly like the illustrations.

METHOD 1

1. Once you have determined the size of the square you need based on your calculations from page 87, place the square wrong-side up, fold in half diagonally, and press. Cut on the fold to yield two triangles.
2. Arrange the two triangles, right sides together, matching the two A edges. Be sure both tips extend beyond the corners exactly ¼" so that the crevice to begin sewing is ¼" from the edge. Pin and sew with a ¼" seam allowance and press the seam open. Notice the extended tips and where they are; do not trim them off.

A

B   B

A

Cut diagonally.

Crevice →   A A

Pin and sew.

¼"

¼"

Detail

3. Using a ruler, mark a 7"-8" line the width of your desired cut bias. Cut up the line about 4". Mark an X to the right of the cut and up at the top of the seam.

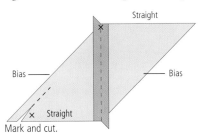

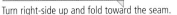

Mark and cut.

4. Turn the piece right-side up. Fold both B edges to the seam.

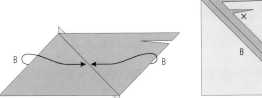

Turn right-side up and fold toward the seam.

5. To be able to sew the last seam, which makes the tube from which you will cut the continuous length of bias, bring the X's up to each other, right sides together. The two X's tell you the approximate areas to align and sew. However, you are not going to match these X's to each other.

Now align and pin the two B straight-grain edges so the extended tips (rabbit ears) are level with each other. At this point the fabric piece will seem awkward and unruly and look very odd. Just keep going. When the seam is sewn it will look like and be a tube. Continue to align and pin the edges. The opposite end of the seam from the rabbit ears will have the fabric on top extend beyond where the fabric underneath ends. Stop sewing when you no longer have two pieces of fabric.

Tips are level.
Left end of seam

Match straight-grain edges and pin.

Right end of seam

Stop sewing at end of double thickness.

6. Press the seam open. Leave the tube wrong side out and if it is large enough, place it over the narrow end of your ironing board. Continue to mark the bias width with a ruler and scissor-cut around the tube until complete. You could also rotary cut the bias by inserting a small rotary cutting mat and using a ruler and rotary cutter.

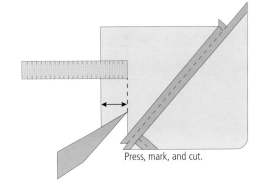

Press, mark, and cut.

METHOD 2

1. Repeat Steps 1 and 2 from Method 1.
2. Mark cutting lines, parallel to the bias edges, the cut width of your binding. Also, mark a line on the straight-grain edges exactly ¼" from the edge by aligning the ¼" line of your ruler just off, but touching, the edge of your fabric to allow for the width of the marker.
3. Align the two straight-grain edges, right sides together, offsetting them by one binding strip width. The ¼" line will help you to now align, match and pin appropriate lines together exactly. Sew the seam with a ¼" seam allowance. When the seam is sewn, check to be sure the lines are perfectly matched across the seam. Press the seam open and cut on the drawn line to create a continuous length of bias binding.

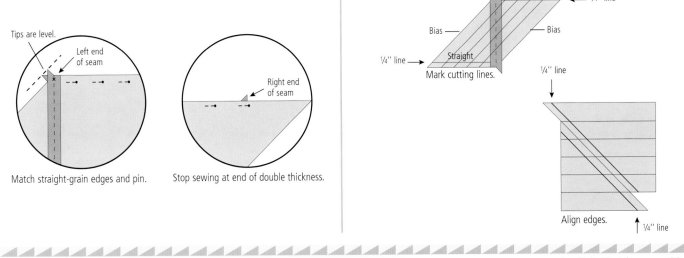

Straight
¼" line
Bias ——— Bias
¼" line ——→ Straight
Mark cutting lines.
¼" line

Align edges. ↑ ¼" line

Individual Bias Strips

1. Once you have determined the size of the square you need, based on your calculations from page 87, and working on your rotary cutting mat so you will not have to move the fabric as you cut, fold the square in half diagonally, wrong-sides together.

2. From the folded edge, continue to make folds evenly toward the point. You are not folding back and forth accordion style but rather folding over and over each other. Do this folding carefully and evenly. The width is not specific. Leave about 1½" from the last fold to the point and pin to hold the folded unit together.

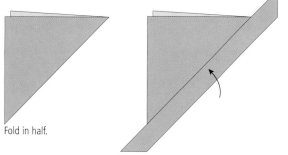

Fold in half.

Continue to make folds.

3. Align the edge of the ruler from the point to the fold, aligning a horizontal line of the ruler on the fold. Cut the folded square into two pieces.

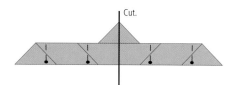

Cut.

4. Cut the desired width of strips from the cut edge of one half, turn the mat, and continue to cut bias strips from the cut edge of the remaining half.

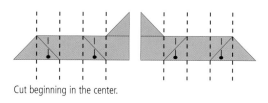

Cut beginning in the center.

5. Join the bias strips end to end, offsetting the extended tips by ¼".

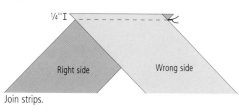

¼"

Right side

Wrong side

Join strips.

6. Press the seam open and trim off the tips.

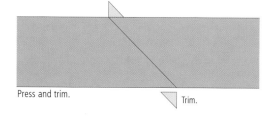

Press and trim.   Trim.

If you are making double-fold binding, carefully fold the bias in half lengthwise, wrong sides together and gently press the fold keeping the iron away from the bias edges. Neatly coil it.

If you are making single-fold binding, mark a line ½" from one raw edge and then bring the edge up to meet the line and gently press. This is the edge that will eventually be hand stitched to the back. Or, you can turn this edge by hand and finger-press, as you hand stitch to the back.

Attaching Continuous Binding

1. Square and baste the quilt. Refer to Preparing the Quilt for Edge Finishing beginning on page 83.

If you are applying continuous binding (bias, straight-grain, single-fold, double-fold) to a straight-edge quilt with corners, lay the binding around the edge or drawn line of your quilt so you can determine if a seam in the binding falls near a corner. If it does, slightly adjust where you begin to avoid excessive bulk accumulating at the corner.

2. To make the beginning point inconspicuous, cut a 45° angle on the beginning tail and leave about 4" unsewn, which will eventually be connected to the ending tail.

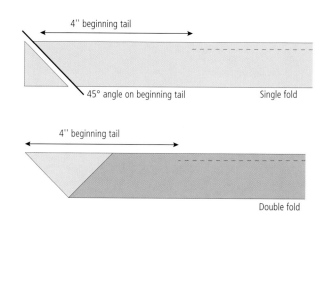

4" beginning tail

45° angle on beginning tail   Single fold

4" beginning tail

Double fold

3. On the right-side edge of the quilt top, beginning about two thirds of the way down, align the raw edges exactly and pin the binding to either the drawn line on the final plain-fabric border or to the edge of the quilt top if the final border is pieced. Be careful not to stretch or pull the binding and use a stiletto to help keep them aligned. Allow the binding to lay comfortably on the edge. Pin and sew a few inches at a time, re-pinning as you go, placing the pins parallel to the edge to reduce distortion and then removing them as you approach.

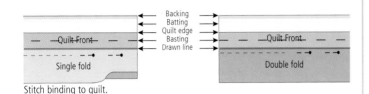

Stitch binding to quilt.

4. Refer to Binding Corners beginning on page 92 for information on corner specifics.
5. Stop sewing about 8" from where you began. Refer to Making the Connection beginning on page 103.

Finishing the Continuous-Binding Edge

Once the binding is sewn to the quilt, the corners are formed, and the ends are connected, trim the backing and batting appropriately, depending on the planned finished width of your binding. Bring the fold (single or double) over the quilt edge to the back and hand stitch in place, just covering the machine stitches.

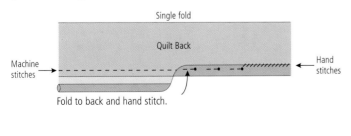

Fold to back and hand stitch.

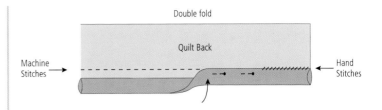

Binding Corners

The corners on a quilt are very important to the final visual impact. Remember wall quilts are for display and viewing, so even one poorly shaped corner will draw the eye and become obvious.

FOLDED MITERED CORNERS

Folded mitered corners are easy to accomplish and give a neat, square, tailored finish to wall quilts. Miters can be created with either double-fold or single-fold binding, straight or bias grain.

To create a successful miter, you must stop stitching the exact distance from the corner as your seam allowance. Decide how you will secure the stitches. You can backstitch, reduce your stitch length to very small, or sew with a regular stitch length, remove the quilt and before you fold the miter, pull up the bobbin thread and hand tie it off.

1. Mark a small dot on the right-side of the quilt top with a pencil or removable marker the exact distance from the corner as your seam allowance width. Insert a pin perfectly straight and perpendicular to the quilt edge you are sewing on.

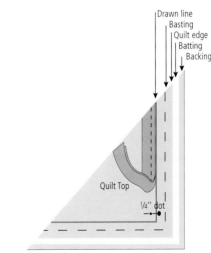

Pin at dot.

2. When the sewing machine needle is side by side with the pin (the miter mark), secure the stitches.

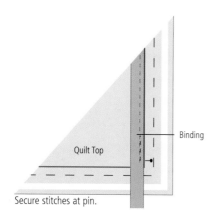

Secure stitches at pin.

3. Remove the quilt from the machine. Fold the binding above the quilt edge creating a diagonal 45° fold and aligning the raw edge of the binding with the edge of the quilt or the drawn line. Secure the fold with a pin.

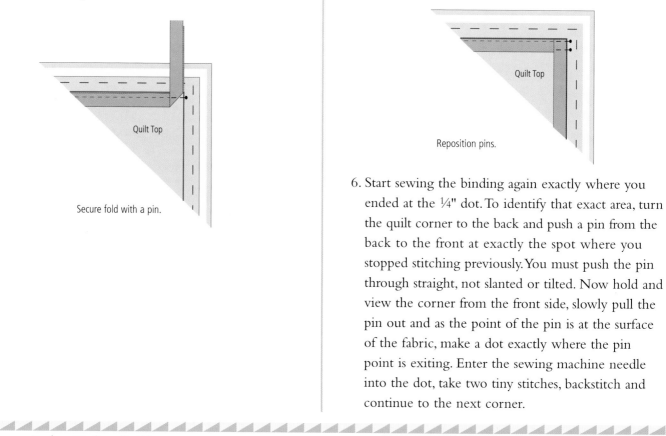

Secure fold with a pin.

4. Bring the binding down to align with the quilt edge or drawn line, creating a fold, which should be positioned exactly at the quilt's top edge or drawn line. This fold must be level. To create a level fold, place your stiletto or long pin at the drawn line or quilt edge and hold it firmly in place as you bring the binding over the pin, which creates a firm stopping point.

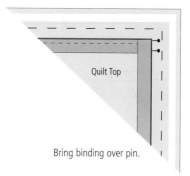

Bring binding over pin.

5. Hold the fold in place with your hand, withdraw the pin that holds the 45° angle, bring it to the top, and re-pin the fold area. When pinning the fold area, just pin deep enough to hold the fold area in place (not through all the layers). If you are sewing with a ¼" seam allowance but creating a wider binding, the fold of the binding is aligned with the edge of the predetermined width of the trimmed batting/backing, not the quilt top.

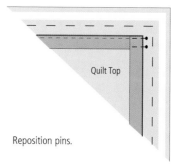

Reposition pins.

6. Start sewing the binding again exactly where you ended at the ¼" dot. To identify that exact area, turn the quilt corner to the back and push a pin from the back to the front at exactly the spot where you stopped stitching previously. You must push the pin through straight, not slanted or tilted. Now hold and view the corner from the front side, slowly pull the pin out and as the point of the pin is at the surface of the fabric, make a dot exactly where the pin point is exiting. Enter the sewing machine needle into the dot, take two tiny stitches, backstitch and continue to the next corner.

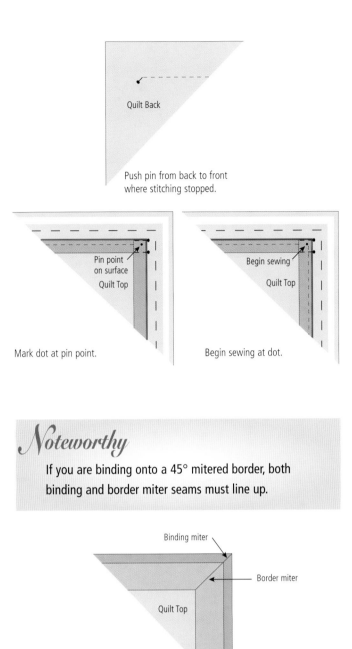

Push pin from back to front where stitching stopped.

Pin point on surface

Quilt Top

Mark dot at pin point.

Begin sewing

Quilt Top

Begin sewing at dot.

Binding miter

Border miter

Quilt Top

Line up border and binding miters.

7. Sew the binding all the way around the quilt, connect the ends, page 103, and trim the excess border, backing and batting to the binding edge.

8. Bring the fold of the binding (single-fold or double-fold) to the back of the quilt to just cover the stitching and hand stitch in place. To form the miter on the back, position your work as illustrated. As you approach the corner, stop stitching about 1½" from the corner. Bring the binding over the opposite edge first, pin, extend the corner to 45°, then bring the binding over on the edge you are stitching and form

the miter; pin in place. Check to be sure it is a 90° corner with a square ruler. Continue hand stitching. When you get to the corner, take a few tiny stitches up the miter, closing the fold, then poke the needle through to the front, stitch down the miter, poke the needle through to the back again and continue hand stitching to the next corner and repeat the process.

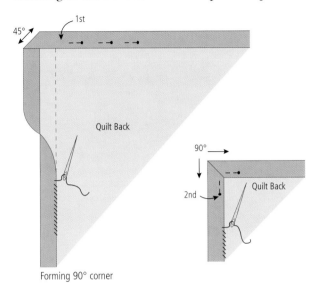

Forming 90° corner

There will be times when you will have corners that are not 90°. The folded miter process can be used on other angles with just a small adjustment. The first fold is the same in that you will stop stitching and secure or backstitch ¼" (or whatever seam allowance you are sewing with) from where the turn should take place.

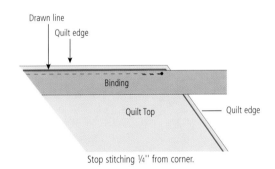

Drawn line

Quilt edge

Binding

Quilt Top

Quilt edge

Stop stitching ¼" from corner.

Remove the quilt from the machine, fold the binding upward so the edge of the binding and the side edge of the quilt or drawn line are aligned and even with each other. Pin to secure the first-fold position. When you bring the binding down, the fold will not align with the quilt top edge but must align with the corner point. The raw edge of the quilt side or drawn line and binding must also align. Start sewing where you stopped, identifying that point as discussed earlier on page 92.

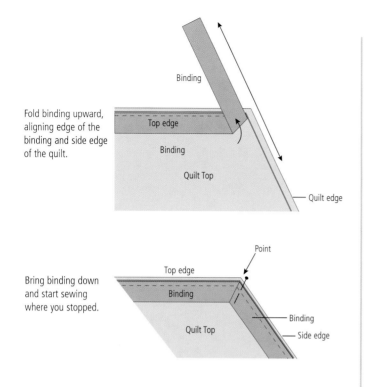

Fold binding upward, aligning edge of the binding and side edge of the quilt.

Binding

Top edge

Binding

Quilt Top

Quilt edge

Point

Top edge

Binding

Quilt Top

Binding

Side edge

Bring binding down and start sewing where you stopped.

ROUND CORNERS

Use bias binding either single-fold or double-fold for rounded corners. Rounded corners are simple to develop and can be a broad or tighter curve. Sketch on paper to see the difference before deciding. The curve can be drawn by tracing around any number of curved objects—plates, glasses, cups, coins, thread spools, and so on—depending on the size of the quilt. Proportion is a consideration. Once you have decided on the curve shape, draw it onto the straight borders and bind to the line before actually cutting the curve. Doing it this way allows you to change your mind.

1. Place the chosen curved object into a corner until each straight edge or drawn line touches the curved object and trace.

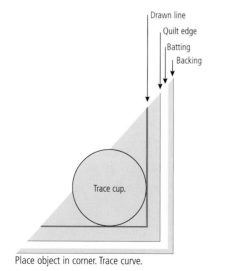

Drawn line
Quilt edge
Batting
Backing

Trace cup.

Place object in corner. Trace curve.

2. Baste just outside the just traced line on all four corners. Do not cut the curve. Align the raw edges of the binding with the quilt edge or the drawn line. Stop stitching a few inches before the corner and pin the bias binding in place, allowing the binding to comfortably lay flat against the quilt.

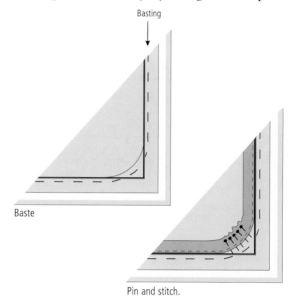

Basting

Baste

Pin and stitch.

Once the binding is completely applied, each corner is carefully evaluated and ends are connected, trim the quilt, batting, and backing to the binding edges and bring the fold to the back and hand stitch in place.

Attaching Individual, Straight-Strip Binding

This style of binding is not a continuous length of binding but rather four individual strips of binding, each applied separately, forming boxed corners. Because the binding strips are added individually, the opportunity to add detail by changing colors/fabrics on each side is an option easily accomplished. It is easier to form the corners with double-fold binding, but there is less bulk with single-fold binding.

1. Measure the quilt horizontally and vertically from drawn line to drawn line or edge to edge, whichever applies; write the two numbers down if a rectangle. If the quilt is square the two numbers should be the same, if not, average them.

2. Cut two binding strips exactly the length measurement of the quilt by the self-determined width including seam allowances. Cut two more strips exactly the width measurement of the quilt plus 2½".

If your quilt is longer than the length of the fabric you are cutting, cut multiple strips and join them diagonally, see page 88, to get the length needed. If using double-fold binding, fold the four individual fabric strips in half lengthwise, wrong sides together, and press.

3. Pin the two length measurement strips to the sides of the quilt, matching the center and ends of the binding strip to the center and ends of the quilt edge or drawn lines. Sew with a ¼" seam allowance. Trim the backing and batting to the binding edge, bring the binding fold to the back of the quilt, pin, and hand stitch in place just covering the machine stitching.

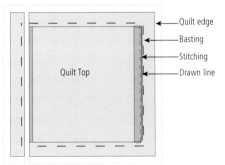

Sew, trim, pin, and hand stitch.

4. Measure in 1" from one end of the remaining binding strips and mark a line. Measure from that line the exact width of your quilt (from line to line is the exact width measurement of the quilt).

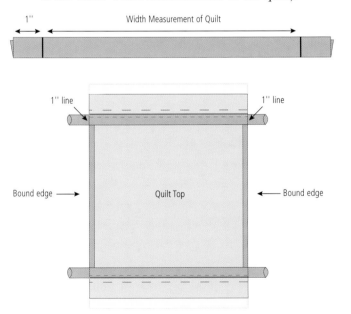

5. Match and pin the center and two 1" lines of the binding strips to the center and two bound edges of the quilt. Sew with a ¼" seam allowance from end to end, backstitching at each end.

6. Mark a line on the binding strip ⅜" from the line at the edge of the quilt and trim.

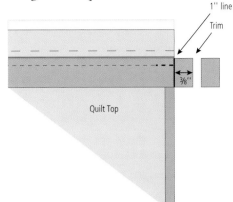

7. Trim backing and batting to the binding edges.

8. Fold in the ⅜" excess even with the bound quilt edge and firmly finger-press, this is a lot of bulk if using double-fold binding. Bring the binding over the quilt edge, carefully forming the corners using a square ruler if necessary, pin corners and edge in place and hand stitch in place.

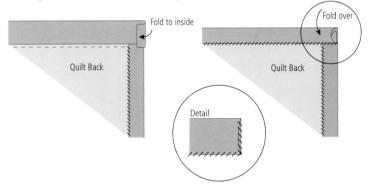

9. Hand stitch the corner fold closed.

Facing

This edge finish works beautifully for existing irregular edges such as a Grandmother's Flower Garden quilt or a Double Wedding Ring quilt, or can be used when you create an irregular edge like curves or scallops. A facing can also be applied to a straight-edged quilt with 90° or rounded corners. A facing can also be used whenever you feel the quilt does not need the added design element of a binding. The final result is an edge that ends with the final border itself. It is not the most durable finish to use on utility quilts but quite appropriate for wall quilts.

Most often, facing is sewn to the front of the quilt from the back and brought to the back. Similarly, if the facing is added to create a decorative shape or edge on the front of the quilt the reverse is true. Obviously, this will influence the color of the facing.

Cutting the Facing

To cut a facing for a small quilt, cut a piece of fabric the size of the quilt and then remove the inner area, leaving a fabric frame. The width of the facing must be wide enough to cover from the edge of the quilt to 1¾" below the deepest crevice of the edge design.

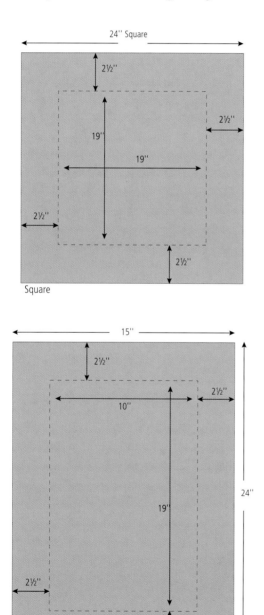

If the quilt is larger than the width of your fabric or if you do not want to waste fabric, create the facing from strips that are joined together to meet the measurements needed. For a larger square quilt with 2½" facing strips, cut two strips the width of the quilt and two strips the size of the quilt length minus two facing widths plus 1" for seam allowances.

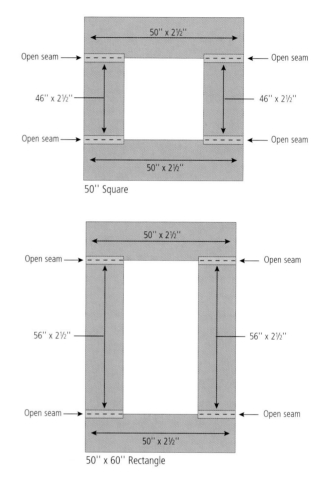

Attaching the Facing

EXISTING, IRREGULAR-EDGE FACING

1. Once the facing has been created and it measures exactly the same as the outer measurements of the quilt, lay the facing on the quilt top, right sides together, align the edges, pin, then baste in place. From the back of the quilt, mark a dot ¼" from the edge at all pivot points. Sew from dot to dot, with a small stitch length, shortening it even further ½" on both sides of each pivot point, all the way around the quilt.

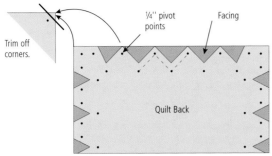

Trim off corners.

¼" pivot points

Facing

Quilt Back

Mark dots and sew from dot to dot.

2. Trim the seam allowance to ⅛", clipping all inside points and trimming off all corner points.

3. Bring the facing to the back, manipulating, and extending all points and corners to form a smooth edge shape. This takes time, be patient. Pin in place as you form the edge. Press, turn under the raw edge of the facing, and hand stitch to the back of the quilt. See Facing on page 95.

DESIGNED SCALLOPED, CURVED, OR IRREGULAR-EDGE FACING

1. Mark the edge shape of the final border on the right side of the quilt.

2. Layer the quilt with the batting and back and baste, with reasonably small stitches, exactly on the marked design line with a thread color that contrasts with the backing fabric. Be sure you can clearly see the design-line stitches on the back and make a mark or dot ¼" from the basting stitches at each crevice so you know exactly where to pivot when sewing. Prepare the facing, being sure the width is adequate to cover from the outer edge of the quilt to 1¾" below the deepest crevice of the edge design.

3. Baste the facing to the quilt top, right sides together, and sew from the back of the quilt, ¼" inside the basting stitches and pivoting at each dot. Use a small stitch length, decrease it ½" on both sides of the pivot points and use a matching thread color.

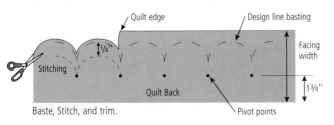

Quilt edge

Design line basting

Facing width

¼"

Stitching

Quilt Back

1¾"

Baste, Stitch, and trim.

Pivot points

4. Trim all seams to ⅛" and clip at inside points. Bring the facing to the back of the quilt along the design line. Turn under the raw edge of the facing and hand stitch.

STRAIGHT EDGES AND SQUARE OR ROUNDED CORNERS

Quilts with straight edges, and square or rounded corners can also be faced using a continuous, straight- or bias-grain single-fold binding (I cut 1⅞" wide for less bulk at corners) or apply double-fold.

1. Make and sew the facing to the quilt as you would if adding binding, but because you will bring the binding completely to the back, mitered corners are developed a little differently. As you approach the ¼" point where you would normally sew to, stop stitching about ½" away from the ¼" point and clip as illustrated.

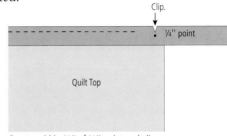

Clip.

¼" point

Quilt Top

Sew to within ½" of ¼" point and clip.

2. Continue sewing with a decreased stitch length to the ¼" point, leave your needle in the mark, lift the presser foot, pivot, and realign the facing edge to the quilt edge or drawn line. Continue sewing 1½", increase the stitch length and sew to the next corner, repeating the process for all corners. Connect the ends as described on page 103.

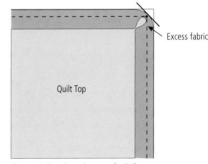

Excess fabric

Quilt Top

Sew to ¼" point, pivot, and stitch.

Noteworthy

With a stiletto or similar tool, redirect and flatten the excess fabric out of the way so as you continue sewing you do not catch any part of it and create a pleat.

3. When facing is applied and ends are connected, clip across the corners and bring the facing to the back, turn under the raw edge, and hand stitch in place forming miters on the back as you normally would for binding. See Facing on page 81.

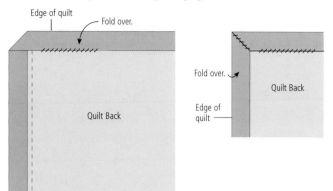

Clip corners, bring facing to back, turn edge under, and hand stitch in place.

Noteworthy

To reduce bulk on the edge, trim the batting close to the seam. If using double-fold, you can also trim one layer of seam allowance.

When adding facing to a straight-edge quilt with rounded corners you must cut bias-grain single-fold facing. You will sew it to the quilt and form the corners as you would for binding. The only difference here is you will bring the facing completely to the back, turn under the raw edge and hand stitch in place.

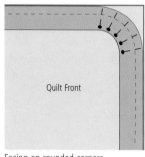

Facing on rounded corners

Prairie Points

Prairie points are folded fabric triangles. They are overlapped at each end by another and sewn to each edge of the quilt. When formed, they are half as tall, from cut edge to point, as the square you start with. They can be formed in one of two ways.

Method 1

Fold a square of fabric in half horizontally, wrong-sides together, and press. Fold both corners down to meet at the center of the bottom edge, press.

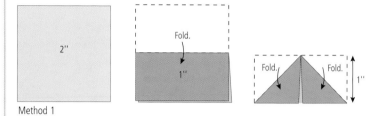

Method 1

Method 2

Fold a square of fabric in half diagonally and press. Fold diagonally again and press.

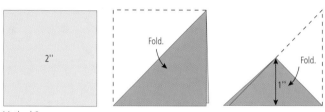

Method 2

Attaching the Prairie Points

Fold the backing out of the way and position and pin a prairie point, right sides together, at the center and both ends of one edge of the quilt top. Continue to position and pin prairie points until the edge is filled, overlapping one on top of the other by about ⅝" (Method 1) or (Method 2) inserting one into the other, making balanced adjustments where necessary.

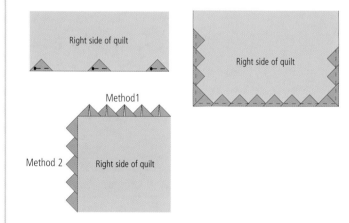

Sew prairie points to each quilt edge or drawn line and batting only, with ¼" seam allowance. Refer to Piping, for finishing.

Piping

Piping creates a fine three-dimensional line of color when placed in front of binding (see *Shadow Baskets* on page 72 and *Hearts* on page 11) or can be used alone as an edge finish, see *Flamenco* on page 41. Whenever piping is used, have it make a statement, be noticed, and contrast with the binding or the final border it is placed next to. Perhaps choose a striped fabric or a very light, bright, or very dark color.

Adding piping to binding creates detail and adds an unexpected but elegant finish. I like to use very narrow ⅛"–¼" nylon cording for my piping because it does not shrink. If you use cotton cording and wash your quilts, preshrink the cording. It's always smart to make up some piping samples of different cording sizes and materials to see what you like best or is most appropriate for your project before making yards of it and then discovering it does not work.

Making Piping

1. Make 1½"-wide continuous bias the length you need, page 88 (this is wider than you need and will be trimmed). Carefully press the bias in half lengthwise, wrong-sides together. Keep the iron away from the bias edges, while gently pressing only the fold. Encourage the bias to fold, don't create a sharp crease. This makes it easier to keep the raw edges aligned while sewing the cording inside the bias and helps to prevent rippling.
2. Lay the cording inside the bias with cording extended beyond the bias edge. It is most important to keep the raw edges aligned and the cording tucked snugly in the fold of the bias.
3. Using a zipper foot, sew next to the cording with a matching thread color. Sew slowly, keeping raw edges aligned. Take your time.

Noteworthy

If you are adding the piping to binding and then to your quilt, you will sew next to the cording a total of three times. If you are adding piping only as the edge finish, you will sew next to the cording twice. Therefore, the initial line of stitching can be ever-so-slightly away from the cording to allow space to sew closer to the piping one or two more times.

4. Trim the seam allowance to ¼" with rotary cutter and ruler. Go slowly, cut accurately a little at a time.

If the piping will follow a continuous curved or scalloped edge on the quilt, clip at ¼" intervals to maximize its flexibility.

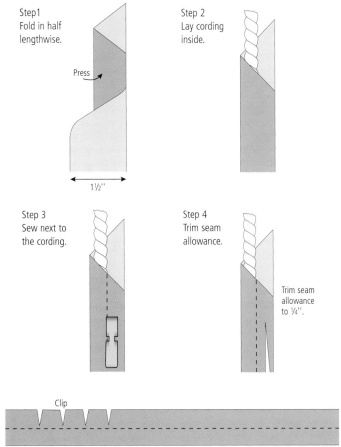

Step 1 Fold in half lengthwise.
Press
1½"

Step 2 Lay cording inside.

Step 3 Sew next to the cording.

Step 4 Trim seam allowance.
Trim seam allowance to ¼".

Clip
Clip seam allowance at ¼" intervals.

Piping on a Large Quilt

Leave about 2" of the border unquilted to allow you to fold the backing out of the way to apply the piping.

1. Fold the backing out of the way. Beginning about two thirds of the way down on the right-hand side of the quilt, sew the piping to the quilt top and batting only, just inside the original stitches (closer to the cording) leaving about a 1½" tail unsewn. See page 92 to complete the corners and page 103 to connect the ends.

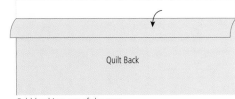

Quilt Back
Fold backing out of the way.

2. Trim the batting close to the seam, and the excess border to the piping raw edge (if piping has been applied to a drawn line).

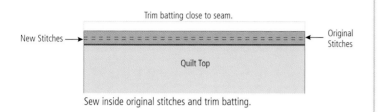

Sew inside original stitches and trim batting.

3. Unfold the backing and smooth it out. Trim the backing to extend ½" beyond the edge of the quilt and piping edges, following any curves or corners exactly.

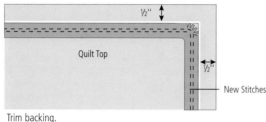

Trim backing.

4. Extend the piping outward away from the quilt so the seam allowance is positioned inward toward the batting. Turn the raw edge of the backing under ¼" and bring the fold over to just cover the machine stitches. Pin in place and hand stitch.

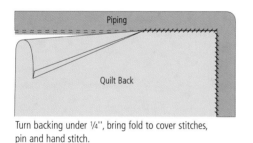

Turn backing under ¼", bring fold to cover stitches, pin and hand stitch.

Piping on a Small Quilt (40" maximum)

If you apply the piping and assemble the quilt layers using the envelope method, the quilting will be done after the quilt edge is finished.

1. Baste the quilt top, right-side up, and batting together, just outside the drawn straight or curved edge line.

2. Prepare and trim the appropriate amount of piping as described on page 99.

3. Align the piping raw edge to the drawn straight or curved line on the final border of the quilt, and sew just inside the existing piping stitches. Do not constrict or pull the piping. Be generous with the piping especially when going around curves and corners, see page 102. Join the ends of the piping, see page 103.

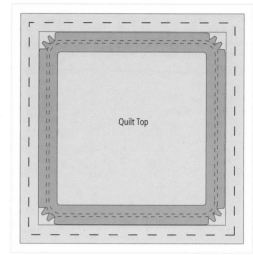

Sew piping to quilt top and batting.

4. Cut two pieces of fabric so the backing is approximately 2" larger than the quilt top and batting after the center seam is sewn. For example, if your batting is 30" square, cut two pieces of backing fabric 32" x 16¼".

5. Place the fabrics right-sides together, and sew a short distance on each end. Press the seam to one side. The unsewn middle section will fold automatically.

Backing fabric

Sew each end.

6. Place the backing right-side up, center the quilt top and batting right-side down. Pin baste.

7. Sew just inside the piping stitches (toward the center of the quilt) all the way around using a matching thread and a small stitch length.

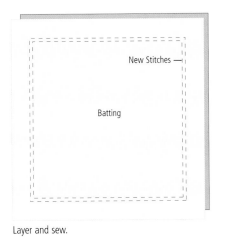

Layer and sew.

8. Trim to ⅛" to ³⁄₁₆" from the stitching line, clip inside and outside curves, if appropriate.

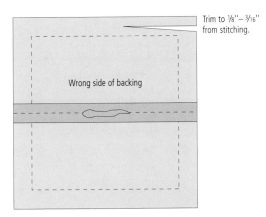

Trim to ⅛"–³⁄₁₆" from stitching.

Wrong side of backing

9. Remove the basting and turn the quilt right-side out. Manipulate and extend the piping outward. This will take time, be patient and form a lovely edge shape.
10. Thread baste about ¼" from the piping on the quilt top through all layers. Hand stitch the backing opening closed.
11. Baste the rest of the quilt as needed and quilt.

Piping Corners

SQUARE CORNERS

1. Mark a dot at each corner of the quilt at the ¼" point and identify that dot with a pin placed perpendicular to the edge you are sewing the piping to.

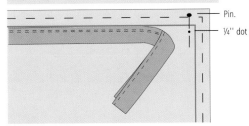

Mark dot and place pin.

2. Sew the piping to the quilt top, just inside the piping stitches (toward the center of the quilt) all the way around, using a matching thread and a small stitch length, stopping about 1" from the corner dot. Clip the piping seam allowance at ¼" intervals ½" before and after the corner dot.

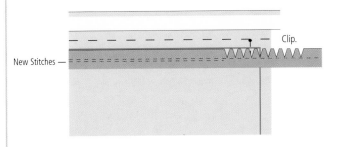

New Stitches —

3. Continue sewing, reducing your stitch length when you reach the clipped area. When the sewing machine needle is side by side with the pin, you will be at the ¼" dot, stop sewing, leave the needle down, turn the work diagonally and take a tiny stitch, then bring the piping edge to align with the opposite quilt edge and continue sewing to the next corner, increasing your stitch length once past the clipped area. This squared corner will have a slight roundness when complete.

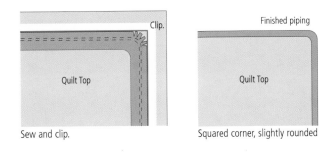

Sew and clip.

Squared corner, slightly rounded

ROUNDED CORNERS

Creating rounded corners with piping is a smooth, easy process and requires bias.

1. See Square Corners, Steps 1 and 2, to stitch the piping to the quilt top. As you approach the corner, stop with the needle down about 2" before the corner and carefully align the piping edge exactly to the drawn line or quilt edge, being generous with the piping and allowing it to lay nice and flat, clipping the piping seam allowance around the corner area only and pinning in place all the way around the corner until the piping edge is aligned to the drawn line on the opposite side of the quilt. Sew slowly, forming a smooth, flat corner.

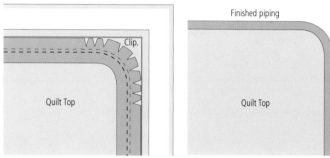

Sew and clip.

Piping/Binding Combination

For this edge finish, make the appropriate amount of piping and bias binding. I recommend a rounded corner for smooth results. Single-fold or double-fold binding can be used. This finish can result in piping and binding both showing from the front of the quilt or, if you bring the binding completely to the back at the seam edge, the binding becomes a facing that is hand stitched on the back, which exposes only the piping on the edge of the quilt. If you do this, trim the batting only, close to the seam line to release some of the bulk.

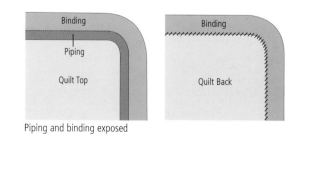

Piping and binding exposed

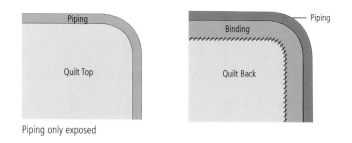

Piping only exposed

1. Sew the piping to the binding with a zipper foot, aligning all raw edges and sewing just inside the existing piping stitches, matching thread to piping, and using a larger stitch length.

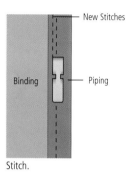

Stitch.

2. Pin the piping/binding to the quilt top, aligning the raw edges of the piping/binding to the drawn line or quilt top edge. The piping will be underneath the binding. Sew with a smaller stitch length, just inside the visible stitches, closer to the piping, beginning on the right-hand side of the quilt about two thirds of the way down. Leave a 4" tail unsewn. Allow the piping to lie smoothly and comfortably around the corners. Stop stitching about 8" from where you began and remove the quilt from the machine.

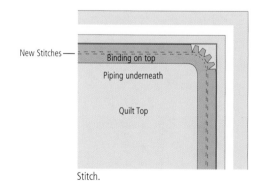

Stitch.

3. Join the ends of the binding/piping each separately. Trim the ending binding/piping tail so it overlaps the beginning tail by 2½". On both the beginning and ending tails, release about 3" of the piping from the binding and pin the two binding tails out of the way.

4. To join the ends of the piping, re-trim the piping ending tail so it overlaps the beginning piping tail by 1". Release 1¼" of the stitching from the ending piping tail only and cut 1" of the cording off. Turn the raw edge under a generous ¼" and finger-press. Insert the beginning tail; the cording ends should touch. Enclose the cording again, aligning all the raw edges. Place piping raw edges to drawn line or quilt edge and pin in place.

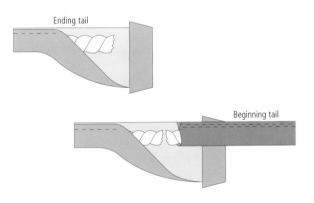

5. To balance the bulk created by the connections, rather than stacking them on each other, the binding ends will be joined past the piping connection. To do that, turn under a generous ⅜" on the ending binding tail and finger-press. Insert the beginning binding tail and trim it so its raw edges are covered. Lay the binding on top of the piping, aligning the edges to the quilt. Sew from where you ended to where you began. It is helpful here to use a stiletto or a seam ripper and lay it snugly next to the cording so you can feel it and can tell where to sew. Do this carefully.

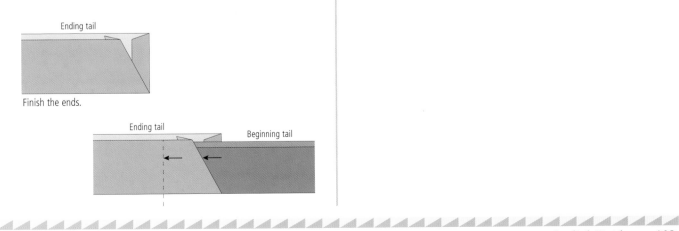

Finish the ends.

6. Trim the quilt top, batting, and backing to the binding/piping edge. Bring the binding fold to the back of the quilt and stitch in place, exposing both piping and binding on the front or the piping only, as discussed earlier.

Making the Connection

Binding

METHOD 1

My preferred method to connect the ends of binding is to sew the two ends together with a 45° seam. This type of connection is easy to do for both single- or double-fold binding, on straight edges and some curves. It eliminates bulk, and is virtually undetectable.

Noteworthy

For clarity, the beginning tail is red, the ending tail is blue, and the thread color is contrasting.

1. Cut the beginning tail at a 45° angle. Begin sewing the binding on the right-hand side of the quilt edge, or drawn line, about two thirds of the way down and leave about a 4" tail unstitched. Sew the binding to the quilt, stopping 8" from where you began.

2. Lay the ending tail next to the quilt edge, or drawn line, and trim off the excess beyond the 8" area between starting and stopping. The ending tail should fill the 8" space but not go beyond it.

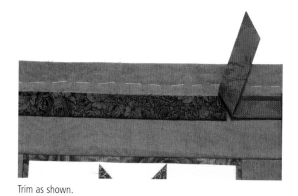

Trim as shown.

3. The first task is to re-create the angle that is on the beginning tail onto the ending tail in the right place. To do that, first notice that the 45° angle on the beginning tail has two points, one long and one short. If connecting double-fold binding, place the beginning tail inside the ending tail so both lay smooth and flat against the edge of the quilt. Where each point touches the inside of the ending tail, make a mark you can see at both points. Be exact; this marking re-creates the angle. Remove the beginning tail, open the ending tail flat, and with a straight edge, connect the marks. You have re-created the angle that is on the beginning tail. To re-create the angle on single-fold binding, lay the beginning tail onto the ending tail and trace next to the cut edge of the beginning tail.

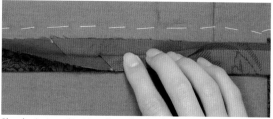

Place beginning tail inside ending tail and make a mark where each point touches the inside of the ending tail.

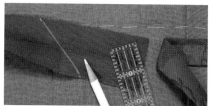

Open ending tail flat and connect the marks.

4. To add seam allowance, place the ½" line of a ruler on the drawn line and draw another line along the ruler's edge. This adds all the seam allowance on one tail. Cut on the last line you drew; be sure you are cutting on the correct line.

Add ½" seam allowance line.

Cut on the last line.

Noteworthy

To bring the two tail ends together for sewing and not struggle with the weight of the quilt, fold the 8" area in the middle and pin, which brings the two ends close together and makes it easier to handle, position, pin, and sew.

Fold and pin to relieve some of the weight.

5. Align, pin, and sew the two ends together with a ¼" seam allowance, being careful not to stretch the bias. Using a ruler, offset the extended points evenly until the crevice is ¼" from the edge. Secure the edge with two or three pins and use a small stitch length and a matching thread color.

Align, pin, and sew.

6. Lay the binding against the quilt edge to be sure it fits perfectly. Then press the seam open, trim off the points even with the edge, repress the fold, align the raw edges to the quilt edge or drawn line, pin, then sew from where you ended to where you began.

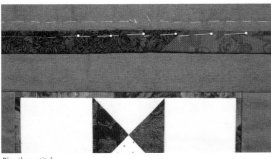

Pin, then stitch.

7. If there is a discrepancy and the connection is a little baggy or loose, re-sew just outside the original stitching to tighten it up. Once it is perfect, remove the original line of stitching, open the seam and continue.

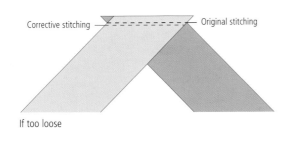

Corrective stitching — Original stitching

If too loose

If the connection is a little tight and constricted, re-sew just inside the existing seam to get back a few threads, remove the first line of stitches, check for fit. If perfect, press the seam open, and continue

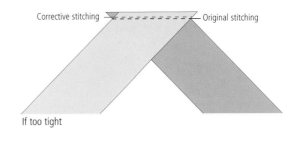

Corrective stitching — Original stitching

If too tight

If you are using single-fold binding, everything is similar only easier. Because there is no fold, you simply lay the beginning tail onto the ending tail to re-create the angle. Then add the ½" seam allowance and continue, beginning with Step 5.

METHOD 2

This method applies to both single- and double-fold binding. After you have cut a 45° angle on the beginning tail, turn the edge under ¼" and press. After you have sewn the binding around the quilt edge, stopping 8" from where you began, trim the ending tail at 90°, being sure it is long enough that the raw edges will be well covered when inserted into the beginning tail. Finish attaching the binding to the quilt. When you bring the binding to the back for hand stitching, you must also hand stitch the folded connection closed.

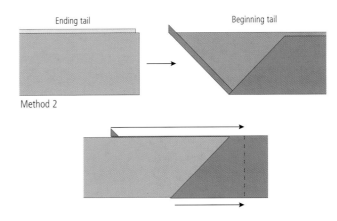

Ending tail   Beginning tail

Method 2

METHOD 3

This method is sometimes appropriate when using single-fold binding on tight curves and is the method I use when joining ends on the piping/binding combination. The beginning and ending tails both maintain a 90° angle. Once the binding is sewn around the quilt edge, stop sewing 8" from the beginning point. Overlap the beginning tail with the ending tail by 1" and cut. Turn under the edge of the ending tail about ⅜", insert the beginning tail into it, being sure the raw edges are well covered and finish attaching the binding to the quilt. When you bring the binding to the back of the quilt for hand stitching, hand stitch the connecting fold closed.

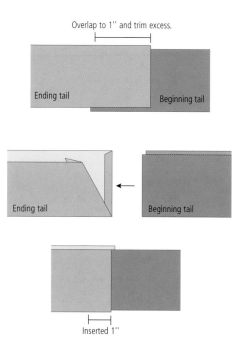

METHOD 4

This method is the same as Method 3 except you will actually sew the ends together rather than folding and inserting one into the other, which will create far less bulk. Once you have sewn the binding around the quilt edge and stopped 8" from the beginning point, overlap the beginning tail with the ending tail by ½" and cut. Now align, pin, and sew the two edges together with a ¼" seam allowance; press the seam open.

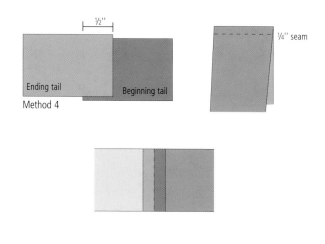

Piping

Refer to Piping/Binding Combination beginning on page 102 for instructions on how to connect the ends of piping.

Curved or Scalloped Edges
Designing the Curve

Inspiration for a scalloped or curved edge can come from many places. I have a French writing desk that has a beautifully shaped edge. Quilting stencils are another good source for shapes, or look at books or magazines. Ornamentation on; or the shapes on the edge of a frame might inspire you; or perhaps a beautiful, ornate rug. The edge can be a symmetrical, undulating, gentle curve, or a repeated scallop. An asymmetrical edge could be designed by sketching on paper from the center to the corner for a square quilt and when mirrors are placed at the corner you will see the complete design. On a rectangular quilt, sketch or draw from the center of a short side around the corner to the center of a long side. Mirrors placed appropriately will again allow you to see the complete design.

Your design might begin by folding a square of paper in half diagonally, then scissor-cutting a curved edge, which when opened allows you to see how a corner would look, or dividing the space into an equal number of divisions, or paper folding. The design process for an edge shape is the same as designing appliqué curves, vines, and so forth. Refer to Appliqué Borders beginning on page 33.

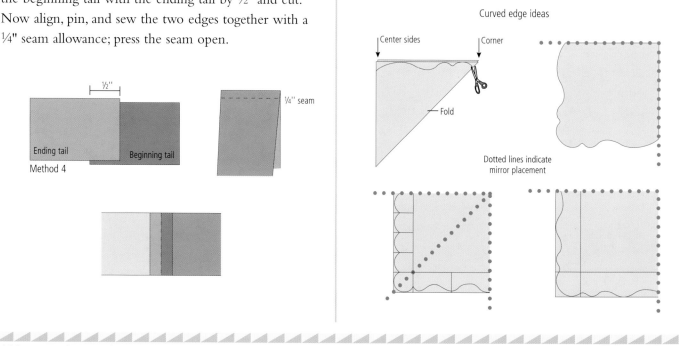

Curved edge ideas

When designing scallops for your quilt, you need to consider the depth of the curves and how far from the outer edge of the quilt the deepest valley will be. Divide the side of the quilt into an equal number of divisions and then trace a curved object (cup, glass, plate, etc.) to create the scallop shape. Consider how deep the crevice or inside point will be, as well as its angle. The sharper the angle the more challenging it will be to bind or face.

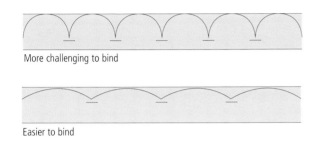

More challenging to bind

Easier to bind

Binding the Curved Edge

Bias binding is necessary to go around the curves smoothly.

Once you have designed an edge, transfer the design line to the final border of the quilt top. When the quilt is layered with the batting and backing, hand baste just outside the line using reasonably small stitches. The raw edges of the bias binding will align exactly to the drawn line when applying the binding. Apply the binding slowly, pinning it in place and allowing the binding to lie flat on the edge and around the curves. On undulating and gently curved edges, no clipping will be needed in most cases. If clipping is necessary, clip the binding seam allowance only, not the quilt edge.

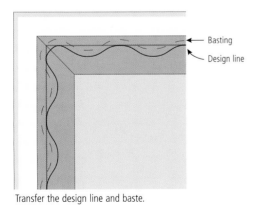

Basting

Design line

Transfer the design line and baste.

Binding the Scalloped Edge

1. Transfer the design line to the quilt border and mark the pivot points ¼" from each crevice.

2. Pin binding around the curve to the pivot point. Sew one scallop at a time. Leave a 3" tail and begin sewing (¼" seam allowance) about 1" before a crevice. Sew to just in front of the pivot point. Stop at each pivot point, clip at the inside crevice to release the binding, and pivot. Be generous with the binding. Lift the presser foot, pivot half way and make a small horizontal stitch across the pivot point mark, clip the seam allowance on the binding only, then bring the binding edge in alignment with the next scallop edge, sew a few stitches, and stop. Pin to the next pivot point and repeat the process. Sew with a reduced stitched length about ½" on both sides of the pivot point. Do not cut the curved shape until the binding is applied and meets your standard. Use Method 3 or 4 on pages 105–106 to connect the ends of the binding, depending on how severe the angle is. Then trim all layers to the binding edge, bring the binding to the back, and hand stitch in place. Depending on the sharpness of the crevice angle, a miter fold will automatically form on the front and broaden out as you bring the binding to the back for the hand work.

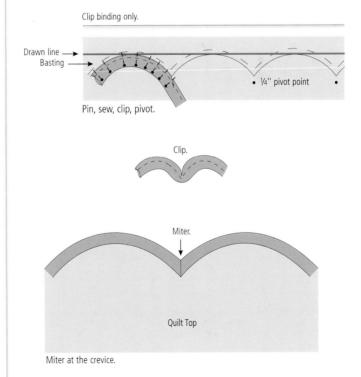

Clip binding only.

Drawn line

Basting

• ¼" pivot point •

Pin, sew, clip, pivot.

Clip.

Miter.

Quilt Top

Miter at the crevice.

SELF-CREATED FINISHES

Bringing the Backing to the Front

Bringing the backing fabric over the batting to the front and hand or machine stitching in place creates this self-bound finish. Although this edge finish is not as durable as applying a separate binding, it is an acceptable technique if done well. Obviously, you want to have a coordinating color/fabric for the backing when you use this technique. This style of finishing is appropriate for straight-edged quilts with squared corners.

Boxed Corners

1. If you have not quilted to the edge, baste around the quilt ¼" from the edge by hand or machine through all three layers. This basting is important to compress and stabilize the edge.

2. Lay out the quilt and trim the batting and quilt top even with the drawn line (see pages 83-84), being very careful not to cut the backing fabric.

3. You must now decide how wide you want the self-binding to be. Trim the backing fabric so it extends beyond the quilt edge twice the desired finished width of the self-binding. Do this carefully and exactly. For example, if you want ¼" self-binding, trim the backing to within ½" of the quilt top edge with a rotary cutter and ruler.

Noteworthy

If you have piecing to the edge of your quilt, you most likely will require ¼" self-binding.

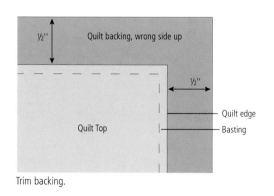

Trim backing.

4. Work on one side at a time, from the center to the corners. Bring the cut edge of the backing to the edge of the quilt top. Be careful to stay straight and not twist the fabric.

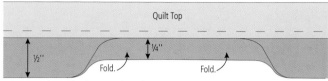

Bring cut edge of backing to edge of quilt top.

5. Bring the fold over the edge and pin in place.

Bring fold over and pin.

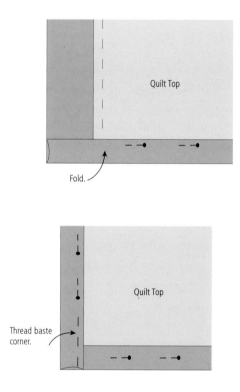

6. Hand or machine stitch in place. Hand stitch end closed.

Mitered Corners

Mitering the corners is the preferred method unless the character of the quilt (Amish style, folk art, primitive, etc.) dictates otherwise.

1. Make a dot on the quilt top at each corner, the finished width of the self-binding from the quilt top edge. Fold the backing corner at a right angle so the fold is exactly at the quilt top corner and finger-press.

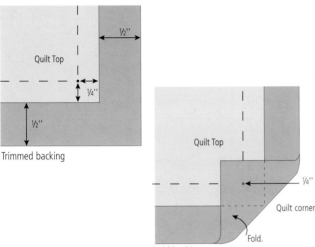

Trimmed backing

Fold backing corner.

2. Fold the point of the corner back until the dot is exposed and finger-press again. Trim on this fold to eliminate the excess fabric that extended beyond the dot.

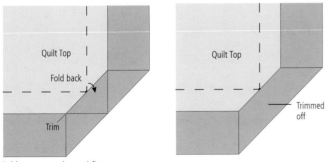

Fold to expose dot and finger-press.

3. Fold in the raw edges of the sides of the backing (one at a time) to the quilt edge, then bring the fold over again to lay on the quilt top to form the miter; pin in place. Hand stitch the miter opening closed, and the folded edge of the self binding to the quilt top.

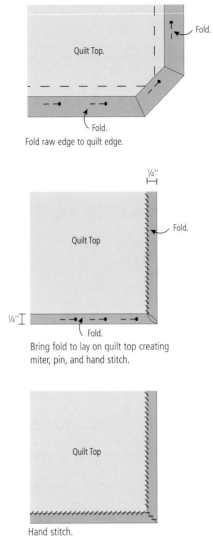

Fold raw edge to quilt edge.

Bring fold to lay on quilt top creating miter, pin, and hand stitch.

Hand stitch.

Envelope or Pillowcase

This is a self-created style of edge finish and is perfect for irregular, curved, or straight edges. You will layer the quilt differently than usual and finish the edge before the quilting is done. This method is appropriate for tied quilts, quilts using loftier batting, and smaller quilts or wallhangings. This edge is not as durable as an applied binding so it is not recommended for bed quilts or utilitarian quilts. For this technique you will have the quilt top squared and cut the exact size plus seam allowance, no excess border. The batting and backing are 2" larger all the way around than the quilt top.

1. Smooth the backing, right-side up on top of the batting, aligning their edges. Place the quilt top, right-side down on top of the backing. Be sure all three layers are smooth and flat. Pin the edges securely and carefully.

2. Beginning with a couple of backstitches about two-thirds of the way down on the right side, sew around the quilt top edge with a ¼" seam allowance using a matching thread and a small stitch length. Use an even-feed foot or feature for smooth sewing. Stop sewing 10" to 20" (depending on the size of the quilt) from where you began stitching and backstitch.

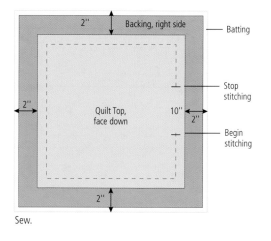

Sew.

3. Trim the batting and backing to the quilt top edge. Re-trim the batting only, another ⅛" to release additional bulk. Trim square corners.

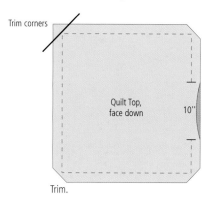

Trim.

4. Turn the quilt inside out through the opening, manipulating and forming good edges and corners. Hand baste ¼"–½" from the edge to stabilize. Hand stitch the opening closed using a matching thread and tiny stitches. Quilt as desired.

Noteworthy

If scalloping or curving the edge, mark the curved line on the right side of the last border, then hand stitch exactly on that line with small stitches and a contrasting color of thread you can see from the back. Use that thread line as a reference for sewing.

Knife Edge

Knife edge is a self-created edge finish wherein the quilt top and backing are sewn together by hand. It will be important to stop quilting ½" from the edge or drawn line on the quilt. This is not a durable finish but adequate for wall quilts.

1. Trim the quilt top and backing ¼" larger than the finished quilt size. Trim the batting approximately ⅛" shorter than the quilt top and backing.

2. Fold the quilt top edge down ¼" and over the batting. Fold the backing ¼", aligning both folds. Pin or baste.

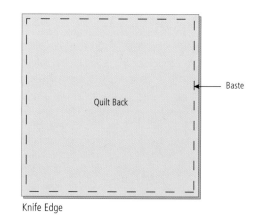

Knife Edge

3. Hand stitch the folds together, forming well-shaped corners. Machine sew ¼" from the finished edge with a straight, curved, or decorative stitch and an even-feed foot or feature.

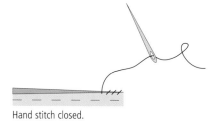

Hand stitch closed.

INDEX

ABOUT THE AUTHOR

Photo: Joe Collins

Sally Collins is an award-winning quiltmaker, teacher, and author who took her first quilting class in 1978 and quickly discovered the pleasure and joy of making quilts. Although she is most recognized for her quality workmanship and teaching expertise, her continual love and interest is in the process of quiltmaking, the journey. She loves the challenge of combining design, color, and intricate piecing in a traditional style. Through this book, Sally hopes to guide and encourage quilters through the process of successfully designing, fitting, and applying borders, bindings, and edges to their own quilts.

Sally spends her time traveling across the country conducting workshops and giving lectures and enjoying life with her husband Joe; son Sean; daughter-in-law Evelyn; and grandchildren, Kaylin, Joey, and Lucas. Workshop and lecture inquiries can be sent directly to Sally Collins at 1640 Fieldgate Lane, Walnut Creek, California, 94595.

Bibliography

Browning, Bonnie K., *Borders and Finishing Touches,* American Quilters Society, Kentucky, 1998

Craig, Sharyn and Harriet Hargrave, *The Art of Classic Quiltmaking*, C&T Publishing, California, 2000

Dietrich, Mimi, *Happy Endings*, That Patchwork Place, Washington, 1989

Dunn, Sara Sacks, Editor, *Fantastic Finishes*, Rodale Press, Pennsylvania, 1999

Fons, Marianne and Liz Porter, *Quilters Complete Guide*, Oxmoor House, Alabama, 1993

Jones, Owen, *The Grammar of Ornament*, Dover Publications, New York, 1987 (Originally published by Day and Son, London, 1856)

Kime, Janet, *The Border Workbook*, That Patchwork Place, Washington, 1997

Martin, Judy and Marsha McCloskey, *Pieced Borders*, Crosley-Griffith, Iowa, 1994

Mazuran, Cody, *A Fine Finish*, That Patchwork Place, Washington, 1996

Peters, Paulette, *Borders by Design*, That Patchwork Place, Washington, 1994

Schneider, Sally, Editor, *Sensational Sets & Borders*, Rodale Press, Pennsylvania, 1998